History of Education for the Twenty-First Century

The Bedford Way Papers Series

1 *Music Education: Trends and issues*
   Edited by Charles Plummeridge
2 *Perspectives on School Effectiveness and School Improvement*
   Edited by John White and Michael Barber
3 *Education, Environment and Economy: Reporting research in a new academic grouping*
   Edited by Frances Slater, David Lambert and David Lines
4 *Exploring Futures in Initial Teacher Education: Changing key for changing times*
   Edited by Andy Hudson and David Lambert
5 *50 Years of Philosophy of Education: Progress and prospects*
   Edited by Graham Haydon
6 *Men as Workers in Services for Young Children: Issues of a mixed gender workforce*
   Edited by Charlie Owen, Claire Cameron and Peter Moss
7 *Convergence and Divergence in European Education and Training Systems*
   Andy Green, Alison Wolf and Tom Leney
8 *FE and Lifelong Learning: Realigning the sector for the twenty-first century*
   Edited by Andy Green and Norman Lucas
9 *Values and Educational Research*
   Edited by David Scott
10 *The Culture of Change: Case studies of improving schools in Singapore and London*
   Peter Mortimore, Saravanan Gopinathan, Elizabeth Leo, Kate Myers, Leslie Sharpe, Louise Stoll and Jo Mortimore
11 *Education and Employment: The DfEE and its place in history*
   Richard Aldrich, David Crook and David Watson
12 *The Maths We Need Now: Demands, deficits and remedies*
   Edited by Clare Tikly and Alison Wolf
13 *Why Learn Maths?*
   Edited by Steve Bramall and John White
14 *History of Education for the Twenty-First Century*
   Edited by David Crook and Richard Aldrich

History of Education for the Twenty-First Century

Edited by
David Crook and Richard Aldrich

Bedford Way Papers

INSTITUTE OF EDUCATION
UNIVERSITY OF LONDON

First published in 2000 by the Institute of Education, University of London,
20 Bedford Way, London WC1H 0AL
www.ioe.ac.uk

Pursuing Excellence in Education

© Institute of Education, University of London 2000

British Library Cataloguing in Publication Data:
A catalogue record for this publication is available from the British Library

ISBN 0 85473 619 0

Design and typography by Joan Rose
Cover design by Tim McPhee
Page make-up by Cambridge Photosetting Services, Cambridge

Production services by
Book Production Consultants plc, Cambridge

Printed by Watkiss Studios Ltd, Biggleswade, Beds

Contents

List of contributors		*vii*
Introduction		
David Crook and Richard Aldrich		*ix*
1	Publicizing the educational past	
	Gary McCulloch	*1*
2	History, education and audience	
	William Richardson	*17*
3	Net gains? The Internet as a research tool for historians of education	
	David Crook	*36*
4	Finding our professional niche: reinventing ourselves as twenty-first century historians of education	
	Wendy Robinson	*50*
5	A contested and changing terrain: history of education in the twenty-first century	
	Richard Aldrich	*63*
References		*80*

List of contributors

Richard Aldrich, Professor of Education, Institute of Education, University of London
David Crook, Lecturer in Education, Institute of Education, University of London
Gary McCulloch, Professor of Education, University of Sheffield
William Richardson, Senior Lecturer in Education, University of Sheffield
Wendy Robinson, Lecturer in Education, University of Warwick

Introduction

David Crook and Richard Aldrich

This volume comprises contributions from five British historians who represent a cross-section of age, academic status and experience. Their dialogue about the past, present and future of history of education began in the summer of 1998 at a British History of Education Society conference held at the Institute of Education in London. Nevertheless, many of the issues addressed by the writers have their own history and have been considered before, for example in the work of Lowe (1983). Other reviews include those by Cunningham (1989), Goodman, Martin and Robinson (1998) and Richardson (1999a, 1999b).

The end of the twentieth century and the beginning of the new millennium provided the occasion for a spate of appraisals and re-appraisals, both in history and in education. One notable feature in the United Kingdom was the appearance of a millennium edition of the *Times Educational Supplement* (31 December 1999). This included contributions by three of the authors in this volume and was planned and edited by David Budge, himself a former Institute of Education MA history of education student.

During the twentieth century, the historical study of education was to be found in a number of contexts. Government reports on education regularly contained substantial historical introductions and history of education became an essential component of teacher training courses. It flourished particularly during the 1960s and remained a central activity of colleges of education and university education departments for much of the following decade. During the 1980s and 1990s, however, the 'disciplines' of education were largely eliminated from courses of initial and in-service training for teachers. Initial training became increasingly school-centred and school-based. In-service courses for teachers also focused upon immediate classroom and managerial concerns. Former teachers of history of education in colleges and departments of education were required to diversify into other areas. Some of these areas were principally concerned with education, for example policy-making and literacy studies. Others were essentially historical in nature, and historians of education made significant contributions to such fields as the history of childhood, both in national and international contexts.

The picture, therefore, was of change rather than decay. For example, throughout the twentieth century, King's College had carried the major responsibility for the history of education within the University of London. With the retirement of Professor Kenneth Charlton in 1983, this responsibility passed to the Institute of Education, where history of education is still taught at Masters and higher degree levels and there has been a succession of externally funded projects. These have led to major publications (Aldrich, 1996; Aldrich, Crook and Watson, 2000). Indeed, the award of substantial and prestigious grants to British historians of education by such bodies as the Economic and Social Research Council, the Leverhulme Trust and the Nuffield Foundation was one of the most significant features of the 1990s.

Thus, in terms of research and publications, British history of education entered the twenty-first century in a relatively strong position. *History of Education*, the flagship journal of the British History of Education Society (founded in 1967 when the discipline was at the height of its fortunes), has recently become a bi-monthly, rather than quarterly journal. The Society's membership has remained encouragingly stable, with a good record of attracting student members who are encouraged, by means of bursaries and other financial support, to attend and participate in the annual conference.

The first contribution to this volume, by Gary McCulloch, contrasts the notions of the 'official' past with 'private' pasts, noting how the latter has become a more powerful determinant of policy-making. As an alternative,

McCulloch calls upon historians to promote a 'public' past, characterized by debate and reflection in the public arena. His confidence in historians of education to lead this debate is not fully shared by his colleague and author of Chapter Two, William Richardson. Richardson's two 1999 *History of Education* articles (1999a, 1999b) offered a wake-up call to British historians of education, some of whom vehemently disagreed with his analyses of the quality and range of writings produced by historians of education based in university education departments. Chapter Two offers a shortened version of Richardson's earlier thesis, but with a particular focus upon audience, or rather the absence of an audience, for many writings in the field. There is much food for thought in this chapter, although some of Richardson's starting points – including his decision separately to categorize 'educationists' and 'academic historians' – are vigorously challenged by Richard Aldrich in Chapter Five. Aldrich argues that education is still developing as a discipline and that there is good reason to believe that historians of education have much to contribute to current and future debates on education.

In Chapter Three David Crook offers some suggestions about how new technologies can help hard-pressed researchers to maximize their productivity and offers a guide to some of the most useful Web pages. Wendy Robinson acknowledges that historians of education may be in need of a makeover, but offers a persuasive case study designed to show how policy-makers in the field of teacher training might benefit from studying the educational past.

It is impossible to predict with absolute certainty the future of research, publication and teaching in history of education in the new century. Nevertheless, we may be sure that such issues as audience, professionalism, purpose, relevance and technology, which are considered in the following pages, will continue to be important. We may also be sure that historians of education must engage in debate about such issues for, as McCulloch notes in Chapter One, 'not to do so means to be marginalized, to be disregarded, to be excluded'. This book is offered as a contribution to that debate.

1 Publicizing the educational past

Gary McCulloch

Introduction

The notion of constructing a history of education for the twenty-first century suggests that educational historians must not only be able to imagine the past, difficult enough though this is in itself. Nor is it sufficient for them to be 'present-minded', for all the criticisms that even such an approach has often attracted (for example Katz, 1987: 1). They must also strive to imagine the future, that is to be futures-minded. This is true for at least three reasons. First, there is the conventional point, widely expressed, that at the start of a new century and third millennium from which so much is expected, we should take stock of our resources and make plans for how we wish to proceed. Secondly, we may hope through such a means to reinvigorate our sense of the past, and to give fresh meanings and interpretations to problems which often seem familiar and even stale. Thirdly, and perhaps most important of all, historians of education are obliged to engage with debates around our present and future in order to maintain a presence, a profile, a voice; for over the last 30 years it has surely become apparent that not to do so means to be marginalized, to be disregarded, to be excluded.

A key theme in this project of orientating the history of education within the new century is to reassess the role of history in helping us to come to terms with educational issues. This in turn entails reconceptualizing the rationale of history of education as a key dimension of educational studies. There are important obstacles in the path to these goals, some of which appear increasingly daunting. At the same time, there are also new opportunities that have arisen in the last few years. In pursuing these, it is necessary to publicize the past in two distinct senses. The first priority will be to raise the profile of the past, to advertise its presence in contemporary concerns. The second will be to render this presence public rather than private or secluded, to turn its face towards a changing society and an impatient world.

Things of the past

Nearly 30 years ago, in the first article of the first issue of the journal *History of Education*, the social historian Asa Briggs set out a general agenda for the study of the history of education. Reading Briggs's article again, one is struck by the confidence of its very first sentence: 'The study of the history of education is best considered as part of the wider study of the history of society, social history with the politics, economics and, it is necessary to add, the religion put in' (Briggs, 1972: 160). This statement serves to define the purpose of many of the finest endeavours of the field over the last generation, and it remains indispensable. Yet, in retrospect, it is no less intriguing for what it omits than for what it includes. While it provides an important endorsement of the history of education as a contribution to the study of history, it fails to explain why the history of education is needed as a contribution to the study of education. In this respect, it did not furnish a rationale that would be able to withstand competing pressures and priorities in a struggle for space and resources. Briggs was not at all unusual in this lapse. For example, in 1966 the leading educational historian Brian Simon could announce that:

> There is no need to make out a case for the study of the history of education as an essential aspect of the course offered to intending teachers. It has long been accepted as such in most colleges and universities and is almost universally taught, in its own right, as part of the education course. (Simon, 1966: 55)

With the wisdom of hindsight, this view now seems to have been unduly complacent. Indeed, there was a need to defend the role of history in such courses, and without this defence it became vulnerable to charges of irrelevance.

Richardson's recent research has shown how the fortunes of the history of education have declined in education departments over the last 30 years (Richardson, 1999a, 1999b). In the light of this, it appears that a major priority for the field in the next 30 years is to defend and assert its potential role in the study of education. Although, as Briggs rightly maintained, historians of education must at all times be aware of what he called the 'broad trends of historical scholarship' (Briggs, 1972: 160), those employed in education departments need to remember and cater for the requirements of their own constituency. Their dual role, as both historians and educationists, will continue to produce tensions as it has in the past, but is not inherently contradictory. It is possible to say, for example, as did David Layton in his fine book, *Science For The People*, that the historical endeavour is useful in order 'to step back occasionally from the ferment of activity associated with present-day problems' and at the same time to try to address 'the striking similarities between many of the issues which engaged science educators in the mid-nineteenth century and those which occupy their latter-day counterparts' (Layton, 1973: 167; see also McCulloch, 1998a). Much excellent and important work has been achieved in the history of education over the last generation, and it remains an exciting and fertile field for further research. Its key problems have been strategic, in conceptualizing and articulating a rationale, in maintaining a base and a constituency, and in locating an audience. Such issues seem more pressing than ever in the year 2000, and are very much unresolved (see McCulloch, 1997a).

In this major project of reconceptualizing the history of education as part of the study of education, as well as of history, several new challenges have emerged in the last few years that make such a prospect appear somewhat remote. First, the advent of the new millennium itself tends to overshadow the past by focusing attention on the future and the apparently limitless possibilities of the twenty-first century, rather than on the experiences of the twentieth century. This in turn exacerbates a tendency which already existed, to ignore the past or to take it for granted, or else to 'telescope' the past in order to draw simple and finished conclusions to particular problems which need to be resolved. Education in the twenty-first century is characteristically idealized in a way that casts aspersions on the failures, disappointments and practical realities of the historical record. It is notable that in the many policy documents on education produced during the 1990s, historical failures were rendered unimportant and irrelevant through a recourse to an idealized future. This would ensure such things as 'equal status for academic and vocational education' (Department of Education and Science, 1991: 24), and teachers who would be 'an authority and enthusiast in the knowledge, ideas, skills, understanding and values to be presented to pupils' (National Commission on Education, 1993: 196), while the 'shabby staffroom and the battered electric kettle' could become 'things of the past' (Department for Education and Employment, 1998a: 13).

It is in this climate of fixation on the future that historians of education must seek to argue for a more substantial sense of history. Yet although this presents a difficult challenge, it also suggests a potential opportunity, for it is in this climate that historical perspectives offer alternative and dissenting viewpoints from those of a prevailing orthodoxy. It may be argued as a counter to millennial futurism that historical appreciation may help to inform our understanding of education, and of the prospects of reform, in the twenty-first century. The contribution of historians of education might be designed as an antidote to current preconceptions, to provide constructive and articulate use of the experience gained in the past, and to allow the hopes and challenges of the twenty-first century to be measured and anticipated as far as possible through this experience.

Another major challenge to history of education in the educational domain is the continuing impact of policy changes and a hostile social and political climate that have combined to undermine its institutional base over the last 20 years. During the 1990s, such pressures if anything intensified further to marginalize and exclude historical approaches in this area. It is noticeable that there has developed among educational researchers an increasing lack of regard for and understanding of historical research. For example, Michael Bassey, in his presidential address to the

British Educational Research Association in 1991, referred to three alternative ways of 'creating education': by playing hunches, through recourse to history or through research. The 'historical way', he asserted, 'entails repeating what has been done before: basing today's action on the way it was done last week or last year' (Bassey, 1992: 3). By contrast, he suggested, basing new developments on research involved 'asking questions and searching for evidence ... creating education by asking about intentions, by determining their worth, by appraising resources, by identifying alternative strategies, and by monitoring and evaluating outcomes' (Bassey, 1992: 3). Such a distinction does a disservice to the potential contribution of historical research in this area, and indeed to the major contributions made by educational historians to the development of education over the last century. It is obviously necessary for historians to make clear to their colleagues in other areas of educational research that their work is also about asking questions, searching for evidence, monitoring and evaluating outcomes, and all the other items in Bassey's list; and indeed that it provides an especially helpful strategy for doing so.

Public criticisms of educational research itself, which grew in intensity in the second half of the 1990s, were generally such as to undermine the position of history even further. For example, Professor David Hargreaves, in his widely publicized Teacher Training Agency lecture in 1996, emphasized the need for educational research to provide direct and tangible improvements in the quality of education provided in schools, and in particular the 'solution of practical problems' (Hargreaves, 1996: 2). Historical research has generally helped to illuminate longer-term problems in their broader social and cultural contexts, and would be unlikely to flourish if the criteria put forward by Hargreaves were applied rigidly. Meanwhile, the Chief Inspector of Schools, Chris Woodhead, has exhibited open hostility to educational research. On the one hand, he has poured scorn on the 'libraries' of books on education which make 'blindingly obvious statements', written in 'a language that is, frankly, impenetrable'. At the same time, he has also argued that this research, while largely responsible for 'many of the theories and beliefs which have guided practice over the last 30, 40 years', many of which in his view 'do not stand up to intellectual scrutiny', is too often 'explicitly ... hostile' to the efforts of government to improve standards in education (Woodhead, 1997: 2–3). Again, these criticisms, while not directed solely at the history of education, have added to the difficulties faced by historians in the educational field. In particular, they have challenged the critical and theoretical basis of the study of education that is a vital foundation for the history of education. Major reports published in the second half of 1998 developed such critiques further by questioning first the quality of educational research (Tooley with Darby, 1998), and secondly the failure of educational researchers to disseminate their work to practitioners and users such as teachers and policy-makers (Hillage, 1998).

Nevertheless, at least some of these contemporary criticisms also offer potential opportunities for historians of education to demonstrate the importance of their work. For example, David Hargreaves complained that whereas in medicine and the natural sciences research was 'broadly cumulative' in building on earlier work, much educational research was 'non-cumulative' in part because, as he alleged, 'few researchers seek to create a body of knowledge which is then tested, extended or replaced in some systematic way' (Hargreaves, 1996: 2). Historians should be on especially firm ground in seeking to counter such a view, as all historical work has a strong conception of previous developments and attempts to theorize how to proceed on the basis of these. Historical research might be said to be profoundly cumulative in the way that it seeks to test, extend or replace existing or previous bodies of knowledge. The potential benefits of historical perspectives on educational issues therefore might be an important feature to emphasize in responding to such criticisms and in seeking to address them.

Historians may also have helpful answers to criticisms of the 'impenetrable' nature of the language of educational research. Woodhead has not been alone in his caustic comments in this area; some educational researchers such as Professor Alan Smithers have also attacked publicly what they see as 'obscure language' that undermines the value of the findings (Smithers, 1995, 1997). Historical writing, however, has generally placed a special emphasis on the importance of clarity and precision of style (for example Gay, 1975), and historians of education may fairly seek to draw on this tradition both to underline their own distinctive contribution and to encourage other educational researchers to pay greater attention to such qualities in their work.

Finding a clear role in relation to the policy agenda of the Labour government elected in 1997 also appears to present a difficult challenge for historians of education. In education, as in other areas, the present Labour government has often preferred to stress the promise of the future rather than dwelling on the past. Once again, however, there are major opportunities for historians of education to address the issues raised in these current policies. For example, *Excellence In Schools*, the major White Paper published in July 1997 soon after the election of the Labour government, based its prescriptions for the future on an explicitly historical argument about what it called the 'deep and historic roots' of contemporary problems in education. It suggested that, unlike in many other industrialized nations, the importance of mass education had been neglected in England and Wales at the end of the nineteenth century, and that it was only slowly recognized during the twentieth century. Thus, according to the White Paper, while these other nations 'recognised that a strategy for national prosperity depended on well-developed primary and secondary education for all pupils, combined with effective systems of vocational training and extensive higher education', in Britain 'mass education was neglected, and governments were content to rely on private schools to provide the elite entry to universities and the professions' (Department for Education and Employment, 1997: 10). Therefore, it insisted that this historical tendency needed to be countered by emphasizing 'the needs of the many, not just the few' (Department for Education and Employment, 1997: 11). The set of policies that have been developed on this basis demands further historical leverage to be applied over the next few years, so that new initiatives such as 'Education Action Zones' and 'literacy hours' can be related clearly to earlier efforts to promote the 'needs of the many'. It is important also for historical analysis to assess the prospects for success of these new policies, that is to base assessments of these policies upon historical experience.

In the same way, the Green Paper *The Learning Age*, published in 1998, emphasized the unprecedented demands of the 'new age', in which 'familiar certainties and old ways of doing things are disappearing' (Department for Education and Employment, 1998b: 9), but also invoked historical arguments to support its proposals. For example, it contended that 'We are fortunate in this country to have a great tradition of learning. We have inherited the legacy of the great self-help movements of the Victorian industrial communities ... . Learning enriched their lives and they, in turn, enriched the whole of society.' In accordance with this tradition, it is asserted, 'The Learning Age will be built on a renewed commitment to self-improvement and on a recognition of the enormous contribution learning makes to our society' (Department for Education and Employment, 1998b: 8). Historians of education should again be able to evaluate such claims and also develop other potential linkages with this 'great tradition of learning'.

In the context of the educational and social reforms being put in place by the Labour government, more broadly, an emphasis on social and cultural issues in education seems to be coming to the fore that was much less apparent in the 1980s and early 1990s, and this tendency may also generate new opportunities for historical research. After all, as Charles Webster observed in 1976:

> Historical reconstruction is likely to be an embarrassment if educational mechanisms are framed in cost–benefit terms, whereas past experience assumes an obviously fundamental importance if education is seen as a means of fostering social cohesion and the critical awareness of the people. (Webster, 1976: 190)

To the extent that such basic purposes are currently being contested, in and around policies for further and higher education for example, historical analysis may be an especially valuable means of understanding the dilemmas that are confronted, and the solutions that are framed. Support in pursuing such understanding can come from the most unexpected of sources, such as Chris Woodhead who in a widely noted piece in the *New Statesman* concluded a standard assault on the excesses of educational research by suggesting that 'the future lies, if it lies anywhere, in the rediscovery of the importance of historical perspective ... and above all, in a return to what was once the classical terrain: issues, that is, concerning social class and educability and schools as social systems' (Woodhead, 1998).

In many ways, then, despite the decline in the position of history of education over the last 30 years and the apparent difficulties of the present position, there are many opportunities for historians of education to involve themselves in current debates and to demonstrate the value of their potential contribution. It is this that constitutes the first general means of publicizing the past: simply to advertise and broadcast as widely and clearly as possible the distinctive claims of historical perspectives, to raise their profile as an important and effective yet too often neglected approach to understanding and addressing the problems of today.

Towards a public past?

In reconceptualizing the history of education for the twenty-first century, it is helpful to draw a distinction between three different types of educational past which are probably always present to some extent, are interwoven and yet have their own separate and distinct histories. These may be described as the 'official' past, the 'private' past, and the 'public' past.

The first of these types of educational past, the official past, was especially prominent in the United Kingdom from around the 1920s until the 1960s. It involved the State and its agencies transmitting a simple version of the past to help to rationalize the growth of the education system, the gradual progressive reform of this system, and the development of the teaching profession. This general version of the past was constructed around a liberal notion of steady, gradual evolution towards social improvement. It expressed a set of shared values through which existing developments would be continued into the future. This kind of outlook was reflected vividly in the major official reports of the Board of Education's Consultative Committee in the 1920s and 1930s, under Hadow (1926 and 1931) and Spens (1938). It was endorsed further in the reports of the

Central Advisory Council on Education from the 1940s until the 1960s, in particular Crowther (1959), Newsom (1963), Robbins (1963) and Plowden (1967). It helped to sustain public support for further educational development and for the teaching profession. In relation to teachers themselves, both in initial and in-service training, it provided an inspiration and purpose for their work.

According to the Hadow Report of 1926, on the education of the adolescent, for example, the problem of making effective provision of education for children between 11 and 15 years of age 'has behind it a history extending back almost to the beginning of public education in England, and it has given rise, particularly in recent years, to more fruitful educational activity' (Board of Education, 1926: 70). Therefore, it continued, 'It is on the basis of the experience thus obtained that further progress will now be made.' Indeed, it concluded, 'The question is not one of erecting a structure on a novel and untried pattern, but of following to their logical conclusion precedents clearly set, and of building on foundations which have long been laid' (Board of Education, 1926: 70). Over the following 40 years, the reports of the Consultative Committee and then of the Central Advisory Council sustained an official image of the educational past, both with respect to specific issues and for the education service as a whole. History of this liberal and progressive kind was incorporated and ingrained in State education policy, both validated by it and contributing actively to it. Lengthy historical sections, for example in the Spens Report of 1938 and in the Crowther Report of 1959, provided a central basis for the policy prescriptions that followed.

Since the 1960s, however, the 'official past', or at least this version of it, has largely gone into eclipse, together with the source that had been mainly responsible for its manufacture. The impressive series of reports that had been produced by the Central Advisory Council came to an end, and most if not all official documents on education produced from the 1970s onwards showed little concern for the historical context of current issues. In part, this was because the increasing pace of policy change hardly allowed for the leisurely production of reports over 2 or 3 years. The discipline imposed by the general election cycle meant that fresh agendas and solutions were required on a regular basis, in addition to the need to respond quickly to particular problems as they arose. Therefore, official history was a victim of the policy overload of the 1980s and 1990s. More profoundly, its precipitate decline came about as its story of gradual progress unravelled. By the 1970s, its celebration of a progressive past contradicted the reality of the lived experience of too many teachers, parents and politicians for it to be sustained further. Confidence in existing 'precedents' and 'foundations' began to look too much like complacency. This took place also in the context of a more general loss of confidence in the idea of gradual social improvement, and the beginnings of a public reaction against the Welfare State and social planning that was to find its strongest political expression in the Conservative governments of the 1980s. The shared values on which earlier reforms had drawn became less clear, and social progress was called into question (McCulloch, 1994, 1997b).

In the 1980s, it might be argued that 'official' history was regenerated in a radically different guise to support new policy priorities and convictions. This was the antithesis of the liberal-progressive version of the past that had been so potent a generation before. History became a story of failure and disappointment, even of betrayal. It was seen increasingly as part of the problem, as an explanation of failure, rather than as the basis for solutions. A hostile, negative view of history as the enemy of an improved future is a striking feature of education policies in the 1980s, representing in many ways an estrangement from the educational past. Ministers publicly endorsed the views of historians of such as Martin Wiener (1981) and Correlli Barnett (1986) to criticize the liberal and academic values of English education, and to blame these for the relative decline of British industry and economic productivity during the twentieth century. The alleged excesses of 'progressive' education sanctioned in particular by the Plowden Report of 1967 were increasingly associated with a purported decline in standards (for example Clarke, 1992). This kind of approach tended to be populist in nature, appealing to the public over the heads of the professionals, again in sharp contrast to the outlook of a generation earlier. Yet this official 'anti-history' lacked some of the properties that had made the earlier version such a significant and durable influence. It did not have adequate machinery to transmit these ideas such as had been available to the Board and Ministry of Education earlier in the century, despite the introduction of a National Curriculum under the Education Reform Act 1988, and the active involvement of successive ministers and even prime ministers in explaining the need for radical policy changes in this area. In particular, it lacked a mechanism for inculcating this notion of history among those who would be charged with putting new initiatives into practice, especially the teachers. It was also subject to open and fierce contestation more clearly than had been the case in the 1940s and 1950s, even within the policy apparatus of the State itself, and certainly in its reception in various parts of an increasingly pluralist and diverse society.

The changing nature and role of 'official history' over the last 60 years raises difficult issues for a reconceptualization of the history of education for the twenty-first century. Its simple and often misleading story lines, its fabrication of convenient myths and its association with the politics of policy formation can all be deeply distasteful and ultimately corrupting. Yet we also know, in hindsight, that 'official history' can help to promote high ideals and aspirations, can motivate teachers by generating a stronger sense of identity and professionalism, and can help to foster a high regard and respect for education among the community at large. In helping to generate an 'official history' for the twenty-first century, historians of education will need to engage actively with the State and the policy-making community, and encourage the development of a usable past. At the same time, they also need to warn of the excesses of official history, and of the problems and complexities that often hide unnoticed and unaddressed behind the simple story line.

The 'private past' in education, by contrast, can be characterized as an individualized, personalized version constructed principally by memory, especially of one's own childhood and schooling, and in relation to one's own family and close circle. Personal memory is always a powerful source of images about the past, and is especially potent in regard to one's own schooldays, childhood and youth. In the 1980s and 1990s, it seemed to have become increasingly prominent as a result of the contestation and general decline of an official past. As an officially sanctioned past lost much of its power to make sense of the present, perhaps personal experience became more important by way of compensation. One of the most interesting ways in which such memories and experiences have been used since the 1970s is by politicians and policy-makers themselves, who have derived and put into action the lessons drawn from their own past. This has often had the effect of raising questions about official ideals of progress, and of signalling disillusionment with general trends and changes.

These personal 'lessons from the past' emerge strikingly, for example, from the published memoirs of James Callaghan, the former Labour Prime Minister, and also of Kenneth Baker, Education Secretary from 1986 until 1989, and Margaret Thatcher, the former Conservative Prime Minister. Each of these enlarges on their own experiences at school, and in Baker's case also on the experience of relatives who had been involved in a growing school system as teachers and administrators, to form a view about the problems of education in the present and how it needs to be changed in the future (Callaghan, 1987; Baker, 1993; Thatcher, 1995). Thatcher's memoirs are especially intriguing in this regard, as they identify four distinct types of view of education held among Conservatives, each of which is based on different kinds of personal and family histories. First, she suggests, there was an important group which consisted of 'those who had no real interest in State education in any case because they themselves and their children went to private schools'. Second were those who 'themselves or their children, had failed to get into grammar school and had been disappointed with the education received at a secondary modern'. Third were those Conservatives who 'either because they themselves were teachers or through some other contact with the world of education, had absorbed a large dose of the fashionable egalitarian doctrines of the day'. Fourth and last, according to Thatcher, were 'people like me', who had been to 'good grammar schools', and who were therefore 'strongly opposed to their destruction and felt no inhibitions at all about arguing for the 11-Plus' (Thatcher, 1995: 157).

Much of this kind of recourse to a private past suggests nostalgia for a lost 'Golden Age' associated with childhood. It may not be too fanciful to see this as helping to fill the vacuum left by the discrediting of the liberal-progressive official past of the mid-twentieth century. In the context of the social and economic policies of the 1980s, moreover, it seems a highly apt development as another kind of privatization, a privatizing of the past, dismantling the official orthodoxies and machinery of the nationalized years, to become dependent on personal convictions and resources (see also McCulloch, 1997b).

As a basis for a history of education for the twenty-first century, memory and personal experience seem highly inadequate and, indeed, dangerous because of the inherent bias and subjectivity involved. It suggests a market place of unresolved and competing views without a shared basis for agreement or common values. Historians of education need once again to point out the dangers of such an approach. At the same time, it is important for them to recognize the resonance of the personal, individual voice. It provides a key source of historical consciousness even for the most historically unaware, and a well of experience that 'official' sources often cannot match. Historians must try to tap into these memories and subjectivities as valuable sources of the past, even at the same time as they warn of their problems and limitations as sources. Personal memory is selective and self-serving, and can generate myths just as effectively as any State apparatus. It is necessary, therefore, to be cautious and discriminating in using memory as evidence or as a basis for action, and to attempt to relate it to other kinds of source, other 'documents' and 'texts', which require just as much careful treatment. There is an important potential role for historians of education in the twenty-first century to conserve and protect the memories of education, without which after all it loses both identity and purpose, but at the same time to mediate and interpret them.

So the official past and the private past both have their roles and both bring dangers, and historians of education can promote and consult in each of these areas. Yet they both seem incomplete without the third kind of educational past to which perhaps especially urgent attention needs to be paid, that is the realm of the 'public past'. This may be characterized as an educational past that is debated and reflected upon in the public arena, through a wide range of channels of communication and media as opposed to the State, but on a more accessible and participatory basis than personal memory would permit. It suggests the possibility of 'publicizing the past' in a second and no less significant sense, that of throwing it open to the public. Such an approach would seek to ensure that the educational past is confined neither to a 'secret garden' of teachers and educators, nor to the 'corridors of power' inhabited by politicians and policy-makers, and that it assumes an important role as part of the learning society of the future.

The public past was probably at its most active and vigorous in relation to education in the United Kingdom in the 1940s and 1950s, generally in alliance with the official past but often in uneasy tension against it, particularly with respect to the continuing social inequalities that tended to lie unremarked in policy documents. The key exemplar was R.H. Tawney, who took a leading part in fashioning public debate about the history of education through a range of channels of information and discussion, at the same time as he was involved in influencing State policy. He achieved this partly through political activity on behalf of the reform of secondary education and over the nature of independent schools, and the Labour Party and the Workers' Educational Association were important vehicles for his work. He also worked through the universities to promote a notion of working-class higher education, and through the *Manchester Guardian* to provide a running commentary and analysis on the contemporary scene that culminated in the Education Act 1944 (McCulloch, 1996, 1998b: 44–56). Other major examples from that period include Fred Clarke, of a different political hue but equally concerned to foster a historical debate about education that would develop in the public arena. Cyril Norwood, although more conservative in his opinions and values than either Tawney or Clarke, was also concerned to generate a historically informed public debate about education in a number of different media. Harold Dent, for many years the editor of the *Times Educational Supplement*, similarly encouraged historical debate as a basis for discussion of the future.

Recalling the public past as an approach to educational history in this way invites us to build on this approach in the twenty-first century, to educate the public about the nature of education, and to provide independent and informed critiques which will challenge received orthodoxies and stimulate debate. It also poses a series of difficult challenges to educational historians themselves, to seek to communicate through clear and straightforward language that can be readily and widely understood, to broaden their horizons beyond the academy and the classroom to the public domain at large, and to make greater use of the new range of media and communications being made available through the new technology (for example Crook, 1999). Overall, it would entail a critical engagement with current issues and problems to shed light upon them using the distinctive skills and insights of the historian.

Conclusions

If we are able to publicize the past by both raising its profile and throwing it open to public debate, it may thereby be possible to make the most effective riposte to the criticisms of Woodhead and others. By this means, we will build on earlier work and develop further a body of knowledge that can be 'tested, extended and replaced in some systematic way'. We will be at the forefront in countering 'impenetrable' and 'obscure' language, from wherever it comes. We will also be well placed to expose the theories and beliefs that have guided practice over the last 30–40 years to intellectual scrutiny.

Such a prospect is a necessary corollary to the vision championed by Asa Briggs in 1972. While retaining an awareness of historical scholarship, historians of education will be no less immersed in the scholarship of education and will demonstrate their commitment to improving education through systematic and critical enquiry. In the twenty-first century, let us strive to recognize our roles both as historians and as educators, in which the study of the history of education may be considered by all means as part of the wider study of the history of society, as Briggs proposed, but just as well as part of the wider study of education, education broadly interpreted with the politics, economics and, it is necessary to add, the religion, put in.

2 History, education and audience

William Richardson

Introduction

Over the last two decades, historiography has moved from the margins of historical writing towards the centre of the stage. Across the English-speaking world, the aggressive challenge of cultural criticism allied to literary theory has put historians on the spot, forcing them to justify their techniques and re-examine their claims. This intellectual 'turn' suggests to historians no mere revision of existing narratives, but confronts them with an assault on narrative itself, especially any narrative claiming to be a truthful representation of the past.

The historiographical literature thus generated is now considerable. Mostly it comprises a technical debate in which professional academics discuss the validity of various methods and aims. One strand of such literature is the uses to which history is put (for example Tosh, 1984), but only rarely within this genre is the question of the audience for historical writing addressed directly (for example Cannadine, 1987). Perhaps this is because, ironically, much historiographical writing lacks an overt historical context. As though forgetting themselves, historiographers seldom explore their concerns through a detailed study of the development in a broad context of the various fields of history. As a counterbalance, this chapter places the audience for historians and educationists in the foreground and considers this theme against the development since 1945 of one distinct field of historical writing: the history of education. In so doing, the intention is to promote a historiography which exemplifies a historically nuanced account of the changing intellectual, political and social contexts within which history is produced.

In considering the changing audience for the history of education and its implications, the chapter opens with a brief account of how historians and educationists in England have conceived their audiences in general terms over the last 40 years. In the process, it is suggested that both groups have paid particular attention to their audience at times of professional opportunity and threat. The chapter then considers the specific audiences in England for the history of education and their changing composition. First, it is noted that in recent years the professional audience has dried up as government priorities have forced teachers and educators to concentrate almost exclusively on immediate policy problems. In response, 'educational studies' in the universities has moved decisively away from the humanities in favour of broadly based social science. In the meantime, academic historians have moved into the space vacated and have sought to redefine the nature and shape of the territory. In the process, they have celebrated the declining influence of educationists over the history of education and set about creating new audiences for the field: students in university departments of history as well as a general readership which includes both 'opinion-formers' and 'ordinary people'. The chapter concludes by anticipating a continued public appetite for the history of education, much of which is produced by groups outside higher education. Within the universities, it is argued that the onus is firmly on educationists specializing in history to put forward a fresh justification of their role and foster a new audience for their work.

Educationists, historians and audience

All teaching staff in universities think about their audience on a regular basis, if only to ensure that the students in their charge attend lectures and seminars and appear to benefit from them. It is not uncommon for newly appointed professors of education or history to use the opportunity of their inaugural lecture to make a personal statement about their vocation, including its audience (for example Howard, 1981; Pring, 1992). Similarly, educationists and historians in England have given more general consideration to their audiences at those moments when there have seemed to be particular opportunities and threats confronting history and educational studies as a whole.

So, for example, the two decades after 1950 seemed to educationists in England a time of great opportunity during which a solution could be found to the elusive problem of defining the basis of their field. During this period, a twofold campaign was advanced. One flank covered the nature of the audience, 'intending teachers' in training; the other emphasized the need for an explicitly disciplinary design for the field as a whole. This dual strategy reaped dividends when, in 1964, the government agreed that expansion in teacher training should be based on an undergraduate degree in which the educational theory comprised four contributing disciplines, including history (Simon, 1990: 134). Against this context, educationists specializing in history asserted in the early 1950s that 'the subject has become not only an integral part of the training course, but a field in which a great deal of research is being done by teachers themselves' and, by 1966, they were claiming that there was no longer any need:

> ... to make out a case for the study of the history of education as an essential aspect of the course offered to intending teachers. It has long been accepted as such in most colleges and universities and is almost universally taught, in its own right, as part of the education course.

The justification, it was argued, was plain: everyone agreed that such subject-matter was appropriate to teacher training courses and many teachers in mid-career returned to the study of discipline-based aspects of education such as history (Armytage, 1953: 47; Simon, 1966: 55).

It was the experience of parallel expansion and change during the same period that led academic historians to a similar re-evaluation of purpose and audience. By 1968, it seemed time to review the 'revolution' that had occurred during the previous decade 'in the structure and scope of university history courses' in England. Despite expansion, it was the compactness of the historical community that was emphasized. For undergraduates 'considerations of personal and school connection, and of the environment, will always influence the choice. Some students may go to particular universities because historians they know may be teaching there' (Harrison, 1968: 357). Yet this homogeneity was coming under strain and the appropriateness of the undergraduate syllabus generated conflicting views between traditionalists who insisted on the centrality of political history coupled to the pedagogy of the Oxbridge tutorial and modernizers who embraced variety, even multidisciplinarity, in university history (for example Harrison, 1968; Elton, 1969: 60–67; Marwick, 1970: 240–242). This debate, seemingly concerned with the interests of the undergraduate audience for academic history, was in reality more about rival conceptions of the professional historian – as generalist or specialist, pedagogue or technician, higher professional or esoteric expert. Moreover, this duality did not serve to differentiate conservatives from radicals as each claimed for themselves aspects of both models of the historian.

Subsequent developments were to reinforce the growing self-consciousness of historians in England about their audience. By the mid-1970s one of the fruits of the 'new' and pervasive social history was the encouragement it gave to radical historians for whom challenging the status quo meant not merely exploring unorthodox subject-matter, but experimenting with historical method, including breaking down the distinction between author and subject. In 1976, the appearance of two new journals provided such an outlet. *Social History* committed itself to being 'iconoclastic, corrosive of received explanations; creative in producing new concepts and devising new methods; and aggressive, encouraging incursions into all fields of historical analysis' (Blackman and Neld, 1976: 1). Meanwhile, *History Workshop Journal* would also be unorthodox, deploying its 'worker-students' on 'the fundamental elements of social life – work and material culture, class relations and politics, sex divisions and marriage, family, school and home' ('Editorial Collective', 1976: 1).

From the outset, *Social History* was committed to eschewing single organizing principles and emphases in social history. A range of explanations and methods was to be integral to its reconceptualization of the field and, in this respect, it represented an early, tentative manifestation in academic history of 'post-modernism' with its implicit rejection of metanarrative (Blackman and Neld, 1976: 1–2). By comparison, its new stablemate *History Workshop Journal* was less bold. The inaugural editorial announced that the journal would be 'a source of inspiration and understanding' with:

> ... a strong grounding in working class experience, but it will also speak from the start to the internationality of class experience ... . We shall try to restore a wider context for the study of history, both as a counter to the scholastic fragmentation of the subject, and with the aim of making it relevant to ordinary people.
>
> ('Editorial Collective', 1976: 1)

However, as international Marxism lost ground, the *History Workshop Journal* gradually loosened its commitment to the monocausal theme in social history. The words 'socialist' and 'feminist' were both removed from the masthead in 1994. Meanwhile, education came under the spotlight and, by 1989, an educationist specializing in history was celebrating the 'important' books the Workshop had produced on the 'deliberate class resistance' of pupils to 'political and economic repression' during the period 1889–1939. Even at this date, however, the same commentator sought to commend the use by History Workshop participants of discourse theory 'to restore ... the working-class voice', apparently reluctant to acknowledge the possibility of conflicting and contradictory voices (Cunningham, 1989: 85–87). Where the *History Workshop Journal* was more clearly groundbreaking from the outset was in its emphasis on collaborative research projects and concern to appeal to a lay readership. Both strands came together in the growth of oral history projects, a research technique which generated a new class of source material while fostering collaboration – both among historians and between historians and their subjects (see Thompson, 1988: 8–11).

By its nature, oral history was confined to recent social history and this limited its influence in the history profession more widely. More challenging was the *History Workshop Journal*'s criticism of scholarly fragmentation and its emphasis on cultivating a lay audience. Both themes were soon resonating in a profession depressed after 1981 by government-imposed cuts and concerned at the supply of history undergraduates from schools (Stevenson, 1993: 66–72). The instinct of conservatives was to look for synthesis and resist an over-specialization which, it was claimed, had cut off British history from 'the large lay audience, the satisfaction of whose curiosity about the national past had once been history's prime function' (Cannadine, 1987: 177). For radicals, the motivation was different. As historians had traditionally 'belonged to the administering and governing classes', their outlook and appeal was unduly narrow; the alternative – a history 'from the underside' which focused on education, labour, the city and the family – was intrinsically a 'more democratic' exercise, capable of reaching new audiences (Thompson, 1988: 3–8).

When contraction came in the early 1980s, historians of all shades were united in an intuitive desire to seek reconnection with a lay public whether this was born of a conservative motivation 'to educate and edify the public' and so win back its respect or a socialist desire 'not simply to celebrate the working class as it is, but to raise its consciousness' (Cannadine, 1987: 178; Thompson, 1988: 20). By contrast, when the basis of educational studies in England came under assault in the late 1970s, educationists had no recourse available to the support of a lay public. From its origins in the Day Training Colleges of the 1890s, educational research had taken one of two main forms: experimental research in aspects of child psychology and cognition directed, in the main, at a technical audience and studies derived from other disciplines (philosophy, history, sociology and anthropology) directed at a professional audience.

Unlike university historians, educationists were used to fluctuations in the size of their profession as higher education staffing mirrored demographic change in the school population. In line with this rule, the dramatic expansion of 'educational studies' undergraduates in the 1960s was followed by an equally dramatic contraction in the 1970s. To compensate, educationists in the universities expanded into higher degree provision via the disciplines-based approach, a model which also strongly influenced the shape of educational research (Richardson, 1999a: 4, 1999b: 110–111, 113). However, the reliance of educationists on the support of national government and the teaching profession made it vulnerable to shifts of political and professional mood and reinforced its inferior status within the universities. It was in this dual context that the 'four disciplines' model of educational studies had been devised in an attempt to win acceptance from fellow academics at a time when the government was relaxed about school standards and keen to elevate the image of a profession compromised by the quality of teacher training offered in colleges of education and validated by the university departments of education (Niblett, Humphreys and Fairhurst, 1975: 152–153, 208).

By 1980, the mood was different. Critics could point to evidence that teacher trainees were most critical of the educational theory component of their courses (Department of Education and Science, 1979: 13), and with school standards climbing inexorably up the political agenda, the university departments of education were forced to change tack. In the face of pressure from Her Majesty's Inspectorate, the local education authorities and, from 1985, central government itself, university educationists reoriented educational studies in a decisive new direction – away from a disciplinary approach and toward practice-based research in which the humanities had little or no place (Richardson, 1999b: 113–114). The option of building a bridge to the lay public was now closed off as educationists gambled on being able to develop a new research tradition which could win the confidence of politicians and a teaching force increasingly unsure of its professional identity. Reinforcing this move was the judgment that in embracing specifically teacher-centred research methodologies (action research and 'reflective practice'), educationists had more to gain from increased dependency on their professional audience than a continued struggle for academic autonomy.

In recent years, it has become starkly clear that the gamble shows no sign of paying off. The outgoing Conservative government and the incoming new Labour government have mounted a sustained attack on university departments of education which is resulting in a significant redirection of funding. Most money for postgraduate teaching in education is now channelled through the Teacher Training Agency and current proposals for reform of teacher training imply the increased allocation of funding to the schools where trainees spend most of their time (Department for Education and Employment, 1998a: 43–53). Some believe that the latter course, if followed, will force many, perhaps most, universities to withdraw from 'educational studies' altogether (Marshall, 1999).

The history of education: audiences past, present ... and future?

If historians and educationists have paid renewed attention to their audiences at moments of opportunity and threat, so too have those specialising in the history of education. The most well-known example is perhaps also the most mischievously argued.

In his celebrated attack on the history of education, Bernard Bailyn of Harvard called for a more sophisticated history of education (Bailyn, 1960: 15–49, 73–114) even as he grossly simplified the historiography of the field into a story of virtue and villainy (Cremin, 1970: 578; Richardson, 1999a: 15). Nevertheless, Bailyn's broadside was far reaching in its influence and around the English-speaking world it has become a commonplace to argue that those educationists who specialized in history during the first half of the century were propagandists intent on idealizing and flattering their professional audience (for example Cohen, 1976; Lowe, 1983). Only in the hands of academic historians, implied Bailyn, could the history of education be safely and fairly appraised for a lay audience. In view of the combative presentation of his case, one important audience for whom Bailyn was writing needs also to be recalled. Anxious to influence government education policy, between 1957 and 1964 the Ford Foundation contributed more than $175,000 to the history departments of leading American universities, including Harvard itself (Richardson, 1999a: 16).

As academic historians warmed to the 'exciting possibilities' that Bailyn (1963: 12) laid in front of them, some were tempted to make explicit his suggestion that it was through academic historians alone that policymakers and the general public could grasp the significance of the educational past. Thus, John Talbott at Princeton declared that if educationists remained in charge of the field it would continue to be 'lopsided' and ignorant of 'some essential facts concerning education itself' which only academic historians could supply. Indeed, such was the complexity of the evidence now being uncovered by academic historians that its assimilation was 'clearly beyond the old-style historian of education and the old-style historiography. But the demands of the task will not be satisfied by a new historiography of education as such', asserted Talbott. Only the 'generalist' historian could 'bring to the study of education a thorough knowledge of the society of which it is a part' (Talbott, 1971: 143, 156).

Educationists and the erosion of audience

Talbott published these remarks in 1971 when interest in a revivified history of education was running high on both sides of the Atlantic. Academic historians were taking an unprecedented level of interest in a field which they had formerly regarded as the domain of dubious educationists. Meanwhile, in the departments of education historical study was securely located in the discipline-based structure of educational studies supported both in America (from 1960) and England (from 1967) by thriving educationist-orientated History of Education Societies. In England Society members had been confident at its inception that the principal audience for the history of education – teacher trainees – could be enthused, although it was acknowledged that the past diet offered to students had often been lamentable (Whitbread, 1968: 4–5). Two avenues in particular were identified for reconnecting this strand of the history of education to its intended professional audience: local studies and liaison with sociology. In the event, neither was particularly successful. As might have been expected, teacher training students were often reluctant local historians and while there was a steady supply of mid-career teachers wishing to research the educational history of their local area, many of such studies were criticized by educationists as being 'extraordinarily conservative – the prototype might be the M.Ed. title "The development of elementary education in the parish of … 1870–1902"' (Batho, 1983: 23).

Equally problematic was the potential liaison with sociology. Some educationists were sceptical that sociology had anything to offer the historian. More commonly such collaboration was tolerated initially, even welcomed; after all, prominent academic historians such as Lawrence Stone had led in this direction. Yet in England, as elsewhere, the difficulty for educationists specializing in history was that, within a decade, they found themselves overrun in their own institutions as educational studies turned its back on the humanities to embrace field-based social science as its core methodology. In the process, both the undergraduate and postgraduate audience for the history of education began to shrivel as standards of teaching and learning in contemporary schools – and how to measure them – became the consuming concern of central and local government (Dent, 1983: 35–37).

As attrition set in, educationists in England specializing in history began urgently to consider the problem of audience, some being provoked into uncharacteristically personal statements about goals and motivation. Peter Gosden, for example, was defiant:

> Part of my own interest in the history of education in the twentieth century springs from a personal desire to find out more about why certain policies came to be adopted and to do this as soon as the material becomes available which enables one to do so with a greater measure of certainty than is provided by ministerial statements, journalists' detective methods, the surveys or deterministic teachings of sociologists and the allegations of contending pressure groups. Thus for me a truly satisfying and satisfactory study of educational policy and administration can only be the historical study when this becomes feasible.
> (Gosden, 1981: 86)

However, as Gosden and his colleagues in the History of Education Society appreciated, defiance alone was insufficient. A conference of the Society in 1982 was devoted to considering the erosion of the field in university and polytechnic departments of education and the views and interests of Society members' core professional audience – 'intending teachers' in training and mid-career teachers on postgraduate courses. The conclusion drawn from surveys especially commissioned for the conference was that the history of education had already been 'losing ground to sociology' in the late 1960s (Dent, 1983: 29–30). By 1977, undergraduate teacher trainees in the colleges of education and polytechnics were voting sociology as the most popular of the 'four disciplines' they were obliged to study, followed by psychology, a state of affairs put down to the greater number of educationists specialising in those fields, the resulting wider range of course options on offer and the preference of students for practical training over less 'relevant' studies such as history (Department of Education and Science, 1979: 12). By 1980, postgraduate teacher trainees in the university departments of education were revealing similar preferences, placing the history of education well behind psychology and sociology in terms both of academic stimulus and professional development (Patrick, Bernbaum and Reid, 1982: 115–116). On the higher degree front, enrolments in historical studies appeared healthy, but History of Education Society members viewed the future with caution. Mid-career teachers might continue to embark on research in the history of education but in an era of contraction the main motivation was likely to be reconciliation to lack of promotion opportunities or early retirement rather than career advancement (Batho, 1983: 20; Gosden, 1983: 17).

Having reviewed the survey evidence, senior members of the Society then proceeded to debate the case for rearguard action in the light of such pressures, a range of justifications being advanced. One suggestion was that students would benefit, whether or not they realized it, from educationists specializing in history researching and teaching the subject on their own terms and for its own sake. On the other hand, and hedging his bets, the same speaker considered that the criteria by which the education department historian judged 'his work and ideas' would benefit from being subjected to 'the continuing experience of presenting the historical approach to those whose chief preoccupation is fitting themselves to go to teach in schools for the first time'. Only one contributor proposed subject-matter that was self-evidently valuable: 'some understanding of the background of the school and its legal status' was required, given that 'from the day a teacher joins a school it is part of his job to help run the school as a community and as an institution'. Otherwise, the historical theme or period was considered of lesser importance than the intellectual development inherent in study of 'the liberalising disciplines' (Dent,

1983: 37; Gosden, 1983: 16, 19). A problem with this line of argument was that the definitions offered and the benefits presumed for such studies were not specific to the pursuit of history. The 'abilities to be critical of the evidence and sensitive of the context' could equally apply to sociology. Similarly, the contention that 'intending teachers' would be assisted in 'developing a clear perspective and in making judgments upon educational debate ... and thus made better professionals in the broadest sense' could be applied to any form of disciplinary study as could the claim that 'an historical perspective' is 'likely to be of greater long-standing use than relatively short-term techniques' (Batho, 1983: 24; Dent, 1983: 37–38).

For History of Education Society members in England the uncomfortable reality of the early 1980s was that, of the disciplinary perspectives offered in educational studies, it was the research techniques of social science that were most in tune with the priorities of politicians and teachers. Thus, within four years of Gosden's defiant apologia, Harold Silver, a leading English historiographer of education, was hinting publicly that the game, as he and others had traditionally been played it, was almost up (Silver, 1985: 2, 4–9). By 1990, the political conditions had become so hostile in England that, as in the United States at an earlier stage, educationists specializing in history had been 'driven decisively from professional and academic roles'. One sign of this was their having 'very largely abandoned the field of recent educational history' to better equipped social scientists (Silver, 1990: 12). Yet in Silver's view, the recent past was the only realistic territory for the 'hesitant historian' in a department of education in England to occupy and his message was stark. They would have finally to bury the hatchet, dismiss 'possibilities of contamination' and collaborate with social scientists: after all, both had 'a shared involvement ... in locating alternative pasts and futures' (Silver, 1985: 4).

The trends outlined by Silver have become more clearly apparent in the intervening decade and are international in their reach. In England, Gosden's ideal of the trained historian in a university department of education 'pursuing his own academic interest through research and teaching' has now itself all but passed into history. Teaching of the subject has virtually disappeared and of those staff surviving almost all combine historical writing (mainly about the recent past) with research projects rooted in the social sciences (Gosden, 1983: 19; Aldrich, 1993: 146). In the United States the History and Historiography section of the American Educational Research Association (established in 1968) is much diminished in size and vitality; in Australia and New Zealand the History of Education Society is fighting for survival (*ANZHES Newsletter*, February 1999).

Academic historians and the cultivation of audience

During the 1980s and 1990s in England and elsewhere the besetting problem facing educationists specializing in history was their dependency on a professional audience which had turned its back on their field in favour of an entirely different disciplinary tradition. Moreover, this was a characteristic which distinguished them from academic historians who, by comparison, have continued to enjoy considerable professional autonomy and share a common academic identity. This is not to deny that 'university history faculties are battlefields where different sorts of history compete for space, each sort equipped with a different methodology and value system' (Clark, 1988: 51). However, what has not been at stake in such faculties is the very survival of the discipline. Over the last decade, historians have discovered sufficient in common to present a broadly united front against the challenge of 'post-modernism' (for example Appleby, Hunt and Jacob, 1994; Evans, 1997), and an important by-product of the repulse has been a deliberate reconnection by leaders of the history profession with a lay audience that has traditionally included leading politicians and other 'opinion-formers'.

Given the relative strength of the two groups in England over the last 20 years, it is hardly surprising that as educationists have relinquished their traditional dominance over the history of education, academic historians have taken occupation of the field and sought to reshape it (Richardson, 1999b: 123–138). Notable in this occupation and reorientation of the field in England is the way in which academic historians have conceived their audiences over the last three decades. In what might be termed a first wave of studies during the late 1960s and early 1970s, individual historians, in time honoured fashion, followed their noses in seeking out interesting avenues of enquiry. To take some prominent examples: Nicholas Orme set out to 'inquire how, in the widest sense, men were educated in medieval times' (Orme, 1973: 1); Keith Thomas sought to expose the 'internal workings of the school' in the early modern period (Thomas, 1976: 4); Lawrence Stone undertook a speculative review of 'the various factors which have influenced the growth, stagnation or decay of education, and especially of basic literacy' during the period 1640–1900 (Stone, 1969: 69); Gillian Sutherland examined elementary education policy between 1870 and 1895 in order to provide 'a case study in the making of social policy in England and Wales during the nineteenth century and a contribution to the history of education' (Sutherland, 1973: 1). At the same time, it was stressed in parallel literature surveys that despite the attentions of educationists over many decades, the field was 'insubstantial' and 'at a primitive stage', so requiring an initial phase of 'tentative and provisional' work. To be sure, education had become 'a respectable, even fashionable subject for study' for professional historians but it was 'still in its formative stages' having suffered from a 'neglect of basic issues' through being 'isolated from the mainstream' (Stone, 1969: 69; Sutherland, 1969: 76; Talbott, 1971: 143; Hurt, 1975: 42; Webster, 1976: 176). The message was clear: historians working mainly on their own and following their intuition would, in due course, refine and promulgate those key themes necessary for a proper understanding of the history of education.

The mid-1970s to the late 1980s saw a second wave. Historians in England publicly celebrated the demise of an historical dimension to teacher training – 'this largely uninspired and unedifying exercise' (Webster, 1976: 176) – and set about consolidating their foray into the field. In addition, joint enterprises began to make an impact. Stone's Princeton seminar on the history of education (1969–1973) concluded with three substantial collections of essays, several history journals ran special issues on education and groups of historians interested in varied aspects of education began to emerge: in the History Workshop, through projects in oral history and via groupings interested in the history of women (Richardson, 1999b: 125, 134–137). Most monumental among collaborative enterprises and symbolic of the traditional interest of academic historians in their own institutions, was the appearance of massive and imposing multi-volume histories of the universities of Oxford and Cambridge (Richardson, 1999b: 125, 134–137).

For over 20 years, academic historians on both sides of the Atlantic had been responding individually and collaboratively to the calls by Bailyn and Talbott for 'generalists' to take up education as a field of study. This gathering of momentum, fuelled by an ever-increasing output of specialist monographs and journal articles, paved the way for a third wave of historical endeavour: the creation of a new genre of study aids and critical bibliographies to symbolize the growing maturity of the field. By the early 1990s, such was the material that had been generated in England that attention turned to disseminating it through evaluative reviews that could perform several functions. The surveys could be used as introductions to the field by history undergraduates and their teachers. They also suggested avenues for further research by postgraduates. In the process, they served to established the main themes in the history of education as these had been redefined by academic historians: education and economic change; higher education and elites; children's work and welfare; technical and scientific education; and childhood in England society (Richardson, 1999b: 134).

The history of education: future audiences?

The steady publication over the last 15 years of volumes in the new Oxford and Cambridge university histories serves as a reminder that since the eighteenth century chronicles of educational institutions have found a ready readership in England. Historians of universities now aim to interpret their institutions in the 'widest context – social, economic, political, intellectual and cultural' (Carter, 1996: 7), but the alumni market for less ambitious studies (albeit to coffee table standards of presentation) shows no signs of abating. Not all have been dismissive of such 'house' histories (for example Thomas, 1976: 5, note 9), but for a majority of professional historians it is, perhaps, their attractive production, authorship by 'amateurs' and respectable print-runs as much as their celebratory tone that rankles. However, the audience for such works is one that is unlikely to go away.

Histories of ancient or elite institutions prompt consideration of how, by way of comparison, the history of 'popular' forms of education is currently celebrated. Here, too, it is evident that the non-professional historian is making much of the running and there is no reason to anticipate a slackening of interest in the oral history of education – often undertaken in schools and increasingly presented on television as well as in print – or diminution of the large number of 'enthusiasts' who reconstruct their own local or family history as it touches on school, apprenticeship or college education (Perks, 1990). This latter trend is in part the fruit of mass education and a culture of early retirement, but it also represents a tangible legacy of movements such as the History Workshop which have sought to broaden the range of those involved in the production of history (Thompson, 1988: 185). In this light, it is indeed ironic that university educationists now find themselves largely excluded from an historical field which in important respects is reaching out beyond the confines of academic history more strongly than ever before. Thus in England two flourishing history of education genres are identified: the 'house' history and 'popular' community-based history of education. Neither one is the exclusive or even dominant preserve of professional historians or educationists specializing in history, yet both seem to have an assured future.

In contrast, what are the prospects for the subject as it is broadly conceived and studied within universities? The current spate of monograph and journal literature surveys on the history of education is but one indication of an expanded profession of academic historians publishing widely in recent social history. Furthermore, the targeting to undergraduates of education as a key theme in economic and social history anticipates the cultivation from among this audience of future doctoral studies, so maintaining or even increasing the momentum. Education is such a central component of both the social experience and State apparatus of industrial societies that it is curious that it took so long for university historians in England to warm to the theme. This reticence seems best explained by their disdain for and disassociation from the work of educationists specializing in history. With the banishment of history from educational studies, academic historians now find themselves able to define the field within the universities on their own terms, unfettered by the requirement to address their work primarily to a professional audience. The result is likely to be further consolidation.

In the meantime, the educationist's voice has not been silenced entirely. Indeed, a further curiosity of the field is the tenacity with which educationists continue to publish journal articles and monographs on historical subjects 'in the presence of overwhelming professional and political pressures' to respond solely to problems in the present (Finkelstein, 1992: 274). In England *History of Education* has more good copy than it can publish and has expanded in size in the year 2000, even though its authorship is the traditional preserve of educationists in higher education, almost all of whom no longer have history of education courses to teach. In America, where the community of history specialists has remained larger and is more used to fighting a rearguard action (Saslaw and Hiner, 1993: 245–263), the response of one group has been to confront the ahistorical nature of education head on:

> ... by portraying a US educational past dominated by an anti-intellectual professional education establishment that has diminished the power and possibility of public education, diluted the integrity of the curriculum, and otherwise fragmented intellectual coherence in schools.
> (Finkelstein, 1992: 275)

That this confrontational approach has been restricted to a 'handful' of radicals (Finkelstein, 1992: 275) serves as a reminder of the relatively circumscribed position of history specialists in English and American colleges and university departments of education. Until the mid-1960s in neither country was there 'a large corps of well-trained historians' in such departments, and even in the boom years historians 'rarely specialized exclusively in the subject' but 'fulfilled other roles in the broader education and training of teachers' (Seaborne 1971: 65–66; Cohen, 1977: 117). The great majority were realists in outlook and intellectual temperament, committed to their role of furthering the teaching profession while at odds with the increasingly ahistorical nature of educational studies, aware that their professional audience was eroding and accustomed to the antipathy of the academic historian (Aldrich, 1993: 141; Saslaw and Hiner, 1993: 257). Most of that generation has now retired and in its place has emerged a smaller, intellectually heterogeneous group. Like many of their predecessors, some of those educationists in England specializing in the history of education double as trainers of secondary school history teachers; others, as Silver anticipated, have attempted in their research to fuse historical scholarship with policy analysis (Aldrich, 1993: 146, 148–151). Others again, more comfortable than the preceding generation with 'theory', have embraced sociological concepts such as 'agency', 'identity' and 'State formation'; yet others – including some with no formal historical training – have adopted life history and oral history techniques (Silver, 1985: 4; Goodman, Martin and Robinson, 1998: 2–3).

This diversity attests to the way in which a scattered yet stubborn group of educationists has adapted to the absence of a student or wider professional audience. Institutionally, their situation is precarious, but motivation clearly remains strong. Perhaps, at some future time, a phoenix will rise from the ashes. If so, one of the conditions necessary will surely be a fusion of the ever-increasing public appetite for popular social history with a new student audience. Within universities the inexorable growth of modular courses could provide a long-term opportunity, especially at the access level and in broadly based part-time degree studies, with the recent history of education being orientated to the family and community experience of mature students.

Less likely in the foreseeable future is a change to the new status quo in research and full-time study, where the history of education is identified primarily as part of mainstream history, presided over by academic historians and aimed at students of history and the lay public. Not only are academic historians tenacious in defending their interests and adept at cultivating their audiences, but staff in university departments of education are currently too far committed to social science methodology and hemmed in by government to foster a career structure in which a significant perspective from the humanities can flourish within mainstream 'educational studies'. In such a situation, educationists specializing in history have no clear constituency or ready audience for their work.

3 Net gains? The Internet as a research tool for historians of education

David Crook

Introduction

British historians of education are now beginning to understand and exploit the potential of the Internet. Already an established tool for acquiring data, it will become ever more important during the next decade. Better-designed Web pages, more sophisticated search engines, faster modems, broadband capacity and the ability to access the Net via digital television and mobile telephones will enable educational historians, both professional and amateur, to access information quickly and conveniently. Going online has recently become much cheaper as a result of aggressive competition for subscribers among Internet Service Providers (ISPs). Several British and pan-European ISPs have now introduced fixed-charge unmetered or free net connections, a welcome move for those who work regularly from home.

Originally conceived by the American military during the 1970s (Barger and Barger, 1998), the Internet did not substantially develop for another quarter of a century. Then, within a 4-year period during the 1990s, it grew from 'an obscure network used by a few universities, to the point at which it had 50 million users' (Puttnam, 1999). It is daily becoming a more important agent for those engaged in formal learning and training. For example, several ISPs have formed partnerships with educational publishers to support pupils preparing for Standard Assessment Tests and public examinations. New 'ask a teacher' electronic mail (e-mail) services are offering help with homework and, shortly, trainee teachers will be required to demonstrate their competence in information and communications technology (ICT) by successfully completing an online test.

This chapter has two main purposes. First, it identifies some useful Internet sites in the hope that some readers will wish to visit them and perhaps add some bookmarks to their Web browser. The hazards of undertaking such an exercise are legion, as Web sites tend to disappear or change address without warning. While each of the hyperlinks included in this chapter was working as the volume went to press, some of them will, doubtless, produce the dreaded '404 Not Found' error message by the time it is published. The second purpose of the chapter is to acknowledge, and briefly to engage with, some of the issues raised by the redoubtable Henk van Setten of the University of Nijmegen. Van Setten's history of education and childhood portal (http://www.socsci.kun.nl/ped/whp/histeduc/) has been – and remains – an inspiration to the present author and to many others (see, for example, Barger and Barger, 1998: 3). A glance at this site, which groups thousands of diverse international Web pages into categories and provides a brief commentary on every link, immediately suggests research possibilities for historians of education and childhood. Although van Setten does not attempt to be independent, indeed he reveals many of his own interests and prejudices and is especially critical of British history of education sites, his Web pages offer an invaluable, non-subscription service to the global community of education historians.

Very little has been written about the relationship between history of education and the Internet. Some historians may still have a sense that the Web is of interest only to a 'geekish' minority of researchers. More typically, however, some functions of the Internet are being used, perhaps even on a daily basis, but without an awareness that the Web is constantly evolving and offering more, both in terms of its content and support for various historical methodologies. Henk van Setten's main interests – and concerns – appear to revolve around the quality of Web content for historians of education. In a useful, if pessimistic, 1998 conference paper for the International Standing Conference on the History of Education (ISCHE) he offered some observations on what he termed the 'Web library':

Let us step back, turn on the lights, and take a closer look at those electronic shelves that are supposed to contain 'History of Education'. What we see is a curious assortment of bits and pieces, from complete books to torn little snippets of paper, from a few dusty cards tied together with a string to neatly bound studies, from hastily jotted-down notes to pretentiously printed brochures: a variety caused by one of this library's peculiar rules: everyone is allowed to dump his or her thing on the shelves, whatever it is. And there is no librarian in sight to keep a neat inventory of all, or at least to tell us what is junk and what isn't. So let's ask ourselves what it is, this curious assortment on these virtual shelves. What kind or kinds of 'history of education' do we have here? What is its use? And should we maybe add something to the shelf?

(van Setten, 1998: 2)

These questions help to frame the organization of this chapter, but an effort is also made to broaden the focus prescribed by van Setten. The Web, it will be suggested, can offer historians of education much more than content. The greatest virtue of many of the sites identified in this chapter, which is likely be of most interest to British researchers, is that they can save some research time. It begins with a guide to some basic Internet functions and then discusses finding aids, bibliographical databases and online sources. Finally, some concluding remarks are offered in respect of technology, historical methodology and professionalism.

Starting out

At present, the most common reason for going online is to send and receive e-mail messages. For the historian of education e-mail offers a convenient and near-instant means of fixing meetings, acquiring factual information and even arranging a last minute archive visit. Modern e-mail applications offer more than a basic messaging service, however. Substantial document attachments can now be exchanged without fear of corrupted text or lost layouts, a feature most keenly appreciated by those who write collaboratively. Similarly, the integration of e-mail and Internet browser software now allows message recipients quickly to access a recommended site by clicking on a hyperlink. Academic newsgroups and e-mail discussion lists have proliferated in recent years. A comprehensive 'list of lists' for UK higher education staff may be found at http://www.mailbase.ac.uk/, while http://edweb.cnidr.org/lists.html is more international in its scope. Some well-supported e-mail discussion groups for historians of education and childhood are now operating. Of these, the H-EDUCATION (register at http://www.h-net.msu.edu/~educ/) and H-CHILDHOOD (http://www.h-net.msu.edu/~child/) discussion lists, both members of the ambitious H-NET Humanities Online Listserv at Michigan State University, are the most active. Both of these groups identify weekly discussion themes, encourage members to pose and answer questions and publish book reviews. The Web is, of course, an ideal medium for free publicity and sales, a point not lost on academic conference organizers, many of whom have abandoned expensive mailshots in favour of Internet sites. For example, in recent years, the Web has been the principal means of advertising the ISCHE annual meeting. Conference participants have been able to submit their papers and abstracts, arrange accommodation and pay their fees online.

The trend for conference information to appear online is, ultimately, likely to be a factor that encourages Web sceptics onto the Internet. So, too, is the lure of cheaper books. Online bookshops have proliferated in the last 3 years, as competitors have sought to claw back the market dominance of Amazon (http://www.amazon.co.uk/), the American-owned pioneer. The leading online bookshops offer a fast service at discounted prices. They boast powerful search engines, permitting customers conveniently to locate and order volumes – gift-wrapped if they so desire – from all over the world. Visitors to these sites unwittingly provide a profile of their interests and spending habits. This is logged by the bookshop's 'intelligent' software and, upon returning to the site, customers are enticed with recommendations and reviews of newly published writings in their specific areas of interest. Whilst the 'big brother' aspect of this may be disconcerting, it should be acknowledged that e-commerce will play an important future part in promoting history of education as a discipline.

The progression from typing Web addresses into a browser to initiating a Web search is relatively simple. The latter can most easily be accomplished by using a powerful Internet search engine, such as Excite (http://www.excite.co.uk/) or Yahoo (http://uk.yahoo.com/). Answers to basic biographical and bibliographical questions can often be ascertained if appropriate search terms are defined. Almost every well-known educationist would appear to have at least one Web site, and often many more, created and maintained by devotees. Unsurprisingly, some of them are poorly designed and contain inaccuracies, while others are obscure or over-theoretical. Henk van Setten's reservations about quality may, however, be over-stated (van Setten, 1998: 4), for there are some hidden gems amidst the 'junk'. Van Setten may also be too dismissive of the Web as a repository for personal testimony. One random Web search, completed in a break from writing this chapter, unearthed a fascinating life story of a nonagenarian female teacher who worked in the same village school for more than 40 years (http://www.rmplc.co.uk/eduweb/sites/billtagg/gladys.html).

Libraries, archives and museums

For academics and students, the facility to search online catalogues in advance of – or even in place of – a library visit, is a welcome technological advance. Similarly, those preparing literature searches for later reading will appreciate the opportunity to print bibliographical records or save them to disk. For scholars at a more advanced stage of their research, remote access to a comprehensive online library can provide such missing details as a publisher or place of publication. The British Library, now physically located in St Pancras, London, offers the most comprehensive UK-based online catalogue (http://opac97.bl.uk), although its current non-availability on Sundays is a disappointment. Of the '24/7' alternatives, the University of London Institute of Education (http://www.ioe.ac.uk/library/librarycatalogues.html) and the Universities of Cambridge (http://www.lib.cam.ac.uk/Catalogues/OPAC/) and Durham (http://library.dur.ac.uk/search/) each boast a comprehensive history of

Net gains? The Internet as a research tool for historians of education 41

education collection and a user-friendly catalogue interface. Thousands of international libraries have an online presence, including the world's largest, the Library of Congress in Washington DC (http://lcweb.loc.gov/catalog//). Links to some 1,400 online catalogues in 62 countries may be found at http://sunsite.berkeley.edu/Libweb/.

The Internet can also help historians to locate primary source archives. Tracking these down can be a time-consuming business, sometimes involving fruitless telephone calls or visits to the National Register of Archives (NRA) in London's Chancery Lane. Help may now be no more than a few mouse clicks away, thanks to the NRA Web pages. The site permits remote searches by personal, corporate or place names (http://www.hmc.gov.uk/nra/abtnra2.htm) and its established series of information sheets, including 'Sources for the History of Education' (http://www.hmc.gov.uk/sheets/4_EDUCAT.htm), can also be downloaded. Search results often reveal hyperlinks to online archives throughout the UK, making the search process both convenient and quick. Further details of the holdings, policies and projects of particular archives can be found at http://www.archivesinfo.net/.

As part of the 'AD 2001 programme', the Public Record Office (PRO) in Kew, London, has recently made available online its entire catalogue of over 8 million document references (http://catalogue.pro.gov.uk/ListInt/Default.asp). Used in conjunction with the very useful printed guide to the PRO's education holdings (Morton, 1997), this service permits amateur and professional historians of education to do most of the important groundwork before travelling to Kew. The PRO has also published Web versions of its Finding Aids, including five dedicated guides to education sources (http://www.pro.gov.uk/leaflets/riindex.htm). Similar developments have occurred at the local level: many county record offices and institutions of higher education have now published detailed online archive search lists.

An innovative resource for researchers – and especially for teachers of educational history – are the virtual education museums, most of which are to be found in America. The Blackwell History of Education Research Museum at North Illinois University (http://www.niu.edu/acad/

leps/blackw1.html) is the most impressive example of the genre. British virtual museums are typically less ambitious, but the Museum of the History of Education at Leeds University (http://education.leeds.ac.uk/~edu/inted/museum.htm), London's Ragged School Museum (http://www.ics-london.co.uk/rsm) and Tom Brown's School Museum in Oxfordshire (http://www.geocities.com/Paris/Rue/1896), each provide Web tasters of actual artefacts. A comprehensive list of school and education museums located throughout the world appears on van Setten's site at http://www.bib.kuleuven.ac.be/bib/peda/archiefc.htm#musea.

Subscription and non-subscription databases

Online library catalogues are an advance for those seeking publication details relating to books, but they do not provide information about published journal articles or theses. Three important databases offering journal information are the British Education Index (BEI), its American counterpart, ERIC, and the Institute for Scientific Information (ISI) Citation Index, all available via the BIDS gateway (http://www.bids.ac.uk/). A database indexing theses accepted for higher degrees by the universities of Great Britain and Ireland, meanwhile, may be found at http://www.theses.com. It should be noted, however, that these are commercial, password-protected subscription services, dependent upon revenues from academic libraries. In practice, therefore, access to these services is likely to be restricted to registered staff and students of subscribing higher education institutions.

Researchers with no institutional affiliation may be interested by INSIDE, a pay-as-you-go Web-based bibliographical database, introduced by the British Library as a rival to BIDS. Readers are permitted to search – and then order and securely pay for by credit card – articles and papers from its unique stock of journals and conference proceedings. Search results are e-mailed to readers' desktops, while the articles and papers themselves can be faxed, posted or sent by courier, according to the customer's preferred price tariff. A rare example of a free bibliographical database is the BEI's index of published articles in the field of vocational education and training (http://www.leeds.ac.uk/bei/vetbib.htm). This site permits multiple search strategies, so articles of historical interest are easily located.

Online bibliographical databases offer great convenience and can be updated more quickly than printed versions. Many historians of education are already benefiting from these services, but some publishers have been quicker than others to publish online. An essential starting point for many historians of education, Chadwyck Healey's Periodicals Contents Index (PCI) to articles in humanities and social science journals from 1770 to 1990, is currently only available to subscribers in CD-ROM format. Those wishing to use this index will, at least for the time being, have to do so in an academic library.

Datasets, e-texts and other primary sources

The arrival of electronic access to primary historical sources promises to add a new methodological dimension to the process of 'doing' research in the history of education. One particularly exciting development is the availability of online datasets, such as the Great Britain Historical Database Online (http://hds.essex.ac.uk/gbh.stm). Constructed by a team of geographers at Queen Mary and Westfield College, University of London, this site offers access to a large collection of nineteenth- and twentieth-century British statistics. Information has been drawn from official reports by the Registrar General and others and relates to such issues as debt, demography, employment, marriage, mortality and poverty. This is potentially a very rich resource for those seeking contextual information about British education.

The PRO, meanwhile, has announced plans to publish the 1901 census online before the end of 2001 (*Sunday Times*, 8 August 1999), while a recently launched project based at the London School of Economics promises to exploit leading-edge technology to publish British official statistics from nineteenth- and twentieth-century Parliamentary papers (http://www.blpes.lse.ac.uk/projects/countess/). To complement these historical datasets, more recent and current statistics, including measures relating to education and other socio-economic factors, are available from the Government Statistical Service (http://www.statistics.gov.uk/).

Several statistical collections associated with funded education research projects are available at the University of Essex's online data archive (http://biron.essex.ac.uk/cgi-bin/biron). Historians interested in pursuing quantitative analyses may also be interested in data gathered for the 1976 annual census of schools, based on 'Form 7' returns – traditionally completed on the third Thursday in January – which form part of the National Digital Archive of Datasets (NDAD) (http://ndad.ulcc.ac.uk/datasets/13/series.htm). These data suggest real possibilities for the future, as do various initiatives of the fledgling History Data Service (http://hds.essex.ac.uk/scripts/releases.idc).

The digital text library is already a reality, thanks largely to the efforts of American volunteers associated with such initiatives as Project Gutenberg (http://www.gutenberg.net/). Thousands of out-of-copyright books have already been digitized and prepared for download, with hundreds more being added each week. Some notable education texts have received this treatment, including Roger Ascham's 1570 manual *The scholemaster* (http://darkwing.uoregon.edu/~rbear/ascham1.htm), John Dewey's 1916 volume *Democracy and education* (http://www.ilt.columbia.edu/academic/texts/dewey/d_e/contents.html) and the original 1912 translation of Maria Montessori's work *The Montessori method* (http://digital.library.upenn.edu/women/montessori/method/method.html). Two useful starting points for British historians of education searching for rare volumes are the Oxford Text Archive (http://www.ota.ahds.ac.uk/ota), which has a strong early modern flavour, and Bibliomania (http://www.bibliomania.com/). In spite of advances in technology and the development of international standards and protocols, the digitization of texts remains expensive, so older technologies may have a currency for a while longer. One British publisher, Primary Source Media, a regular advertiser in the journals of the History of Education Society, has built its business upon sales of entire microfilmed archives and history texts from American libraries.

Historians of recent education policy will be interested in those government and media Web pages that provide access to official documents and the speeches of politicians and others. An online version of *Hansard*, the official record of parliamentary proceedings, at http://www.parliament.the-stationery-office.co.uk/pa/cm/cmhansrd.htm, contains all interactions from both Houses of Parliament, including written answers, since October 1996. The full texts of recent Acts of Parliament and Statutory Instruments are also available from a government portal (http://www.legislation.hmso.gov.uk/). Each of the heavyweight British newspapers has created online archives, although none currently offers material pre-dating the mid-1990s. The *Financial Times* database (http://www.ft.com) operates on a pay-per-view basis, but among the best free sites are those maintained by the *Express* (http://www.express.co.uk/), *Guardian* (http://www.guardianunlimited.co.uk/Archive) and *The Times* (http://www.the-times.co.uk).

The *Times Educational Supplement* has now abandoned its subscription charges and offers a searchable, cost-free archive of articles dating from 1994. Where the dates of news stories cannot easily be authenticated, answers can sometimes be found in the television news archives of the BBC (http://www.bbcfootage.com/) and ITN (http://www.itnarchive.co.uk/). Education Online (http://www.leeds.ac.uk/educol) is another useful site which has already established itself as an important repository of keynote education addresses. Elsewhere, the Department for Education and Employment's press releases, archived to August 1995, shortly after the merger of the former Education and Employment departments (http://www.dfee.gov.uk/newsmain.htm), often reproduce in full or summarize speeches by Education ministers. Transcripts of education speeches can also be found on politicians' own sites, including that of the current Prime Minister. The 'Number 10' pages include a full transcript of Tony Blair's 1999 Romanes Lecture (http://www.number-10.gov.uk/news.asp?NewsId=416&SectionId=32), an incisive and historically informed critique of British education that offers more than the predictable soundbites.

Secondary works and bibliographies

Examples of online versions of published secondary works are rare, but some out-of-copyright examples may be found, including G. Benson Clough's *A Short History of Education* (http://www.socsci.kun.nl/ped/whp/histeduc/clough/index.html). Conference papers – often reporting work in progress – on history of education themes are more plentiful. Education Online has a growing collection of historical papers, among them Greg Brooks' 'Trends in standards of literacy in the United Kingdom, 1948–1996' (http://www.leeds.ac.uk/educol/documents/000000650.htm) and is the official repository for papers delivered at British Educational Research Association (BERA) conferences. Another notable initiative is the Institute of Historical Research's electronic seminar series, which includes a history of education strand (http://ihr.sas.ac.uk/ihr/esh/histedu.html).

Completed research mostly continues to be reported in scholarly journals, which have been quick to seize upon new ICT marketing opportunities. Taylor and Francis, publisher of *History of Education*, the journal of the British History of Education Society, has been a pioneer in offering 'free' Web-based versions of its journals with library subscriptions to traditional paper copies. Access to the electronic edition is often denied to individuals dialling up from home, but the online availability of post-1999 *History of Education* numbers is an undoubted benefit to academics and students working from their offices and research bases. Readers can also sign up for Taylor and Francis's free alerting service and receive via e-mail the contents page of the latest number (http://www.tandf.co.uk/journals/). A wide range of online historical journals, including some with education or childhood slants, may be found at http://www.history-journals.de/ and http://www.tntech.edu/www/acad/hist/journals.html. Most of the journals listed on these sites continue additionally to publish in hard copy, but exclusive online journals are becoming more common. One such American example, Education Policy Analysis Archives (http://olam.ed.asu.edu/epaa/), regularly publishes articles of historical interest.

Barger and Barger have observed that the Web offers considerable scope for 'collaborative learning activities between teachers and students or students and other students' (Barger and Barger, 1998: 2). The number of Internet sites linked to taught courses is certainly growing, but tutors are understandably reluctant to publish online their own course materials. One admirable exception to this general rule is 'A journey through the history of State education in England' (http://panizzi.shef.ac.uk/med/cathy/intro.html), an interactive historical tour designed for undergraduate students of Bretton Hall, Yorkshire. Other sites that may merit a bookmark include Ali Burdon's impressive collection of information relating to the history of British women in education (http://www.sandals.freeserve.co.uk/) and, although ostensibly a site for school pupils, the 'Education, 1700–1950' entries in the Spartacus Internet Encyclopaedia (http://www.spartacus.schoolnet.co.uk/education.htm).

Many higher education institutions are now publishing online course bibliographies. These are easy to update, accessible to students in a variety of locations on and off campus and can produce significant savings in terms of paper, labour and photocopying. Most examples are functional, but some impressive, multi-language bibliographies relating to education in Ancient Greece and Rome may be found at http://bcs.fltr.ucl.ac.be/Educ.html and http://www.uky.edu/ArtsSciences/Classics/ancientschooling.html.

Conclusions

Technology has already changed – and is continuing to change – the way in which historians of education operate, both in the UK and elsewhere. More than ever before, time is of the essence for those pursuing research. In history of education, no less than in any other field of study, project funding – and, indeed, contracts of employment – implicitly factor in the use of the latest technologies. Most scholars already rely upon computers to store notes and data, to wordprocess pieces of extended writing and to exchange e-mail messages. The extent of this dependency may only become apparent when the hardware crashes – as it is prone to do – or when software behaves erratically or fails as a consequence of bugs or viruses.

This chapter has modestly indicated some further possibilities to help hard-pressed historians of education to save time. The ability to locate publication details from online library catalogues or to validate the accuracy of a quote by calling up text from a digital archive will, undoubtedly, redeem many a situation for the home-based researcher or the academic facing an imminent writing deadline. Similarly, the ability to browse archive catalogues in advance of a visit, to list and even order in advance documents of interest, is a highly useful development. The Internet offers much more than this, however. As the British Library has already demonstrated, the prospect of historical documents coming to the researcher, rather than vice versa, is not pie in the sky. Indeed, information delivery on a pay-per-view basis is likely to be an important growth area in the early twenty-first century.

In 1998 Henk van Setten suggested that academic historians of education in 'the ivory tower' were failing to take advantage of opportunities presented by the Internet. Too often, he argued, 'the Web ... is used ... as a replacement for the local notice board in the local university hall, without using its real capacities and potential in reaching the public'. Meanwhile, he argued, some 'amateur' historians of education – including those with high-level Web skills – could be thought of as 'sand dunes', circling the ivory tower with a view to seizing control of the discipline (van Setten, 1998: 5). This interpretation is both over-dramatic and elitist. There is no escaping the fact that some of the most fascinating and useful history of education sites on the Web have no association with academic institutions, but this is hardly a sinister development. The popularity of some recent British television series (Crook, 1999) has shown that educational history – whether at the level of individual life stories, institutional histories or policy trends – has a much broader appeal than universities and their courses are able to address. The Web, too, can play a part in extending the audience for history of education beyond the 'ivory tower'.

In any case, van Setten's concerns about the lukewarm interest of 'professionals' should have been assuaged over the last two years. It is now commonplace for academics and students to conduct electronic searches and to download, rather than borrow or photocopy, some of their reading materials. Commercial publishers and booksellers, meanwhile, are using the Web in various ingenious ways to market and promote the writings of their authors.

If online historians of education can recognize and progress beyond what van Setten terms the 'junk' – usually by asking the same searching questions they would ask of sources presented in any other medium – they will understand that the Web can offer them a great deal. Indeed, it may significantly change their investigative processes and help them to become more productive.

4 Finding our professional niche: reinventing ourselves as twenty-first century historians of education

Wendy Robinson

There was a time when history of education was largely accepted as a necessary and important ingredient in the professional preparation of teachers and in the furthering of academic knowledge and understanding about education. Past educational precedents, practices and experience also featured in major discussions of policy change and reform. This, it could be argued, is no longer the case. The professional niche that historians of education once occupied is now an ambiguous and contested one. History of education as a subject of undergraduate study has largely been excluded from the world of teacher training which it traditionally inhabited. In the realm of postgraduate study, it has to vie with a restricted market obsessed with quality assurance, directly measurable outcomes and financial viability. Its ambivalent location, as it straddles the rival domains of history and education, has rendered it vulnerable to accusations of reduced status, worth and respectability within the academy. The discipline's tenacious association with an uncritical, methodologically unadventurous, 'acts and facts' training college culture has been difficult to shake off, even though it has long moved on from such a narrow remit. In the context of the current political milieu in which competition, accountability, effectiveness and quality have become overriding concerns and education is dominating the agenda for reform, frenzied debates have been muddied with competing aims and objectives over purpose and direction. Mere lip service has been paid to the value of historical perspective (Aldrich, 1996, 1997; McCulloch, 1997b).

Such a legacy of marginalization and status ambivalence might suggest for the discipline a very uncertain future. Yet, at a time of profound and rapid educational change, it is possible that the current prospect may not be as bleak as it might at first seem. We need only turn to the government's recent well-publicized attack upon the educational research community to see evidence for this. Amidst a highly damming critique it is the rediscovery of the importance of historical perspective that is hailed as the only sensible way forward (Woodhead, 1998). As we enter a new century and a new millennium it is both timely and critical for the future of history of education to be reappraised and for its fundamental contribution to educational policy to be reclaimed and recognized. Only when contemporary problems are analysed historically can we understand where they have come from, how certain analogies have been worked out and how they can inform our present. At the same time, it is essential that we prevent the untested myths of our educational heritage from being hijacked and misrepresented to support or uphold specific new policy directives. An embryonic shift in attitude from policy-controllers, combined with the strength of a burgeoning popular interest in matters educational, affords us a valuable opportunity to move into the twenty-first century with a stronger voice, a reconcepetualized professional niche and, in the words of Michael Fullan, the ability to empower ourselves as educators who can become agents rather victims of change (Fullan, 1993: ix).

Whilst this chapter could have highlighted any one of many possibilities for a discussion of the contribution of historical perspective to current educational policy, one very obvious choice, which is also integrally connected with the way in which historians of education might define their own identities, is to target the highly topical and contentious issue of teacher education and teacher professionalism. Having briefly outlined the current position and future prospect of history of education, the discussion will now examine the implications of recent policy reform in this particular field. Changes to initial teacher training, the recent politicization of pedagogy and teaching methods and the effects of such change on teacher autonomy and professional identity will be explored.

A damaging and sensationalized climate of hostility towards teachers and their teaching methods, teacher educators, educational theories and education research in general has characterized recent history. Negative perceptions of teacher education and teacher educators by politicians and the press have become painfully familiar – yet these are all too often grounded in reactionary and presentist terms. With a few notable exceptions (for example Aldrich, 1990a; Gardner, 1993, 1996) so much of the new research and literature on changing teacher education policy and its management at institutional level, lacks any historical perspective. The fact is that so many of the so-called 'new' ideas, debates and areas of contention are not new at all, but form part of an ongoing, long historical continuum which is often overlooked. Teacher education is an area in which historians of education have traditionally operated and in which they are well-qualified and well-placed to make an important contribution. It will be suggested that past models of teacher training, pedagogy and professionalism warrant greater attention because they bear a much closer relation to the current education debate than has previously been given credit. A sharper focus on historical precedent might significantly inform such debate. At the same time, trainee and serving teachers might better understand and appreciate those key professional issues surrounding their work and lives if they have access to a more systematic range of historical perspectives.

First, the key issue of teacher training will be considered. From the mid-1980s, with the establishment of the Council for the Accreditation of Teacher Training (CATE), initial teacher education was subjected to increasingly prescriptive central control. As a policy issue, it became heavily politicized and ideologically driven. In 1994 the Teacher Training Agency (TTA) was set up by Act of Parliament to replace the CATE and to reform teacher training. Throughout this period, the traditional hegemony of college- and university-based provision of initial teacher training has been eroded by a renewed interest in school-based, school-centred, apprenticeship models of professional preparation. The old disciplines of education – history, philosophy, psychology and sociology – which once made up the core of teacher training, have been criticized for their lack of application and relevance to the everyday, classroom-based needs of would-be teachers. Consequently, there has been a rapid deregulation of control of the content of teacher training away from higher education whilst the formal role of schools has been elevated. Theory of education has been marginalized in favour of a greater preoccupation with practical classroom skill and expertise. Experiments with alternative routes into the profession other than the BEd or PGCE, such as the licensed and articled teacher schemes, have stressed the value of on-the-job, school-based training (OFSTED, 1993a, 1993b).

Against a background of relentless educational reform which has focused on school improvement and effectiveness, the quality and ability of the teaching profession has come under increasing scrutiny and suspicion (OFSTED, 1993c; Elliott, 1997). It is teachers, teacher trainers and educational researchers who have been implicated in the perceived decline in educational standards afflicting schools. Teacher training, being the source of future professional staffing for schools, has been targeted as a prime focus for raising school standards, through a well-prepared teaching force. At the same time, however, teacher training which is inappropriately executed could pose a very serious threat and, therefore, greater central control is to be expected.

The recent introduction by the government of a national curriculum for initial teacher training, which prioritizes primary literacy and numeracy (Millett, 1995; Teacher Training Agency, 1996), could be accused of promoting a restricted, instrumental and unreflective approach to professional preparation. It has been decried by its critics (for example Graham, 1996, 1997; Young, 1998) as an overtly technicist curriculum which redefines and ultimately undermines teacher professionalism. Working on the assumption that teacher training has been deeply flawed in the past, the current policy remit, in seeking to raise standards, both in the preparation of teachers and in school effectiveness, has introduced a standards-driven criterion-based model of initial teacher training. Concentrating heavily on skills to be attained and honed in the classroom, it might be suggested that such a model is limiting, with a bias towards short-term professional competence. Such a model leaves little scope for the consideration of those much broader and less tangible educational, theoretical and philosophical issues which might not necessarily be encountered in a particular classroom context. At the same time, an increasingly rigorous system of inspection by OFSTED has been set up to ensure that the TTA's required standards are being met by providers of initial teacher training. Any provider found lacking risks closure or a substantial reduction in its fixed student quota.

Without doubt, teacher training remains a contested issue. Ongoing questions as to the constituents of a professional training, the most suitable locus of expertise, the relative roles of participants and the balance between theory and practice continue to perplex and trouble educationists and politicians alike. In the context of teacher training past and present, any sense of a coherent, consistent or united system of training, in which the various academic, practical and theoretical strands have been successfully reconciled has proved an elusive goal. Yet, if we take a longer view and track the historical development of teacher training over the past 200 years, we can see clearly how those issues raised by recent policy developments have been visited before.

For most of the nineteenth century, professional training had an overriding school-based theme. The pupil–teacher system, which ran along apprenticeship lines, supplied the expanding system of State elementary schools. By the end of the nineteenth century, a refined apprenticeship model, which strove to balance the demands of practice and theory, in partnership with serving teachers and specialists, was being developed. Training colleges offered further training and education to the most able apprentices who, like the trainees of today, followed a State-controlled national curriculum. Contrary to historical 'myth', recent research suggests that by the late nineteenth century, given the particular educational and financial limitations of the time, a systematic and potentially sophisticated form of initial teacher training was being refined and developed at the hands of the teaching profession itself (Robinson, 1997). This was to change at the turn of the twentieth century when teacher training, conflated with secondary education in general and the expansion of higher education, was subjected to the reforms of a Conservative government. Not unlike the current trend, the education of intending teachers came under much firmer central control and supervision. The resulting policy was, however, in reverse to that which has been witnessed recently. Serving practitioners were gradually excluded from the initial preparation and training of teachers and teacher training was subsequently relocated almost entirely in the domain of higher education. With proportionally less time spent learning the skills of teaching in school, greater emphasis was placed on subject knowledge and theoretical perspectives as well as the improved general education of teachers. For the duration of the twentieth century, however, a profound sense of dissatisfaction dogged teacher training. Weighing the cost to practice and school-based skill at the expense of a diet rich in educational theory, generations of government inquiries and reports as well as professional debates analysed and questioned the training needs of teachers against the requirements of schools.

The value of looking back at the patterns which have characterized teacher training – the swing from school-based to higher-education-based models and now back to predominantly school-based models, with varying degrees of convergence along the way – lies not only in the comfort that can be derived from the knowledge and understanding that we are clearly part of an ongoing cycle of change and continuity, but also that this particular cycle of extremes can potentially be broken in the future. From an historical perspective, it is possible to identify and track both simultaneous and linear phases of advance, phases of stagnation and phases of reaction, all of which can inform, enrich and contextualize current developments. Closer historical investigation which looks beyond a narrow interpretation of the development and progression of the teaching profession, to a fresh understanding of those hitherto unexplored moments when advances were briefly made towards a more harmonious and integrated pattern of training, might offer a new dimension to the current debate and point the way forward.

Closely related to issues of teacher training are those of pedagogy and teaching method. Pedagogy, once such a rarely used term in British political, media and even educational circles, has recently featured prominently in discussions about teaching, teacher training and educational research (for example Davies, 1994; Woods and Wenham, 1995). Pedagogy, or the art, science and craft of teaching, is now hailed as the panacea for the perceived inadequacies of the teaching profession and falling standards in schools. For a decade, the National Curriculum has closely regulated what teachers should teach in schools. How teachers have chosen to teach this content has largely been left to professional judgment and individual flair. Now, after years of debate about the appropriateness and value of different methods and styles of teaching, there is a move to ordain the way in which teachers should teach. The literacy hour, for example, which has been operating in all State primary schools since September 1998, is one very obvious expression of such prescription. For many teachers, this encroachment into what officially has been described as the 'last corner of the secret garden' (Millett, 1996) threatens to undermine any remaining vestige of their independent professional autonomy and judgment.

The TTA's increasing concern with establishing a foolproof pedagogical framework has also manifested itself clearly in teacher training reforms, particularly in the new national curricula for ITT. The message conveyed clearly implies that neither the teaching profession itself nor teacher trainers have previously worked within a successful, commonly understood, systematic model of pedagogy. The traditional culture of school classrooms, with lone teachers working behind closed doors, as well as the laissez-faire, discovery-learning approaches adopted by the training colleges, has been blamed for the development within the teaching profession of very private, individualized forms of good practice, method and technique. Since the late 1960s, those heavily dichotomized and often sensationalized exchanges over the relative values of child-centred, whole-class, individual or group teaching methods have plagued educational debates, both within and without the profession. Yet, questions over best classroom practice and teaching method have remained open to question. Against such a damning legacy of the perceived decline in school standards, past teaching methods have been decried as woefully inadequate and fundamentally flawed. Advocates of a new applied science and methodology of teaching, with clear goals and recognized bodies of knowledge, see radical intervention and change as the only solution (for example Reynolds, 1998a,

1998b). No longer can effective instructional methodologies be left to the suspect vagaries of individual schools or teachers. Whole-class interactive teaching based on effectively managed, clearly defined lesson goals, instructional variety and high expectations for all students is now proffered as the best way forward.

As pedagogy becomes increasingly politicized and subjected to a reform agenda which prides itself on its radical and innovatory solutions to problems of teaching method and style, observers might be forgiven for thinking that the whole issue is without precedent or foundation. This situation is not made any easier by the government's loss of faith in the very research community which has, for over 20 years, been striving to address such questions (Mortimore, 1998; Tooley with Darby, 1998). Current political rhetoric wrongly implies that until now any professional engagement with pedagogical matters has either been negligible or seriously misinformed. In seeking to recover pedagogy from its previous neglect, it could be argued that current policy loses much from its myopic disregard of cumulated professional wisdom and understanding built upon a long tradition of experience and research. What is now needed is a more rigorous historical re-evaluation of the role, place and development of ideas and theories around best teaching practice. As well as invigorating and informing current developments, such analysis may uncover hitherto overlooked practices and suggest possible ways forward.

An excellent starting point for this historical re-evaluation of pedagogy is Brian Simon's famous article, published in 1981, entitled 'Why no pedagogy in England?' (Simon, 1981). This article, together with Simon's longstanding research commitment to assessing the constituents of method and good primary classroom practice (Galton, Simon and Croll, 1980; Galton and Simon, 1980; Simon and Willcocks, 1981), reveal a deep concern with the ongoing relationship between theory, practice and pedagogy. Simon has argued a convincing case for the neglect of pedagogy in twentieth-century British educational culture, pointing to a combination of social, political and ideological factors that have prevented the establishment of a truly scientific basis to the theory and practice of education. As such, his analysis resonates with the TTA's present critique.

Yet, what Simon does suggest is that there was once a brief moment in our educational past, when a rigorous and coherent system of pedagogy was being developed and refined by the teaching profession itself. This emergent pedagogical system which sought the systematic integration of theory and practice flourished in the late nineteenth century pupil–teacher centres and training colleges, and gained momentum in the early university day training colleges. It was premised on a positive belief in the innate educability of all children and in the central role of the school teacher to facilitate such a process. The early twentieth-century rise of psychology, psychometrics and intelligence testing, which highlighted and categorized the limitations of human potential, destroyed those earlier pedagogical gains whose roots were found in the lowly esteemed elementary school tradition. This phase of pedagogical development, long historically overlooked, clearly warrants further attention and could make an important contribution to the current policy climate.

Whilst valuable research on the historical development of educational theory has been undertaken (for example Selleck, 1968, 1972), such work concentrates heavily on leading educationists and their theories and fails to explore how such theories were transmitted to the profession and how they were implemented practically in schools. Clearly, there is scope for further research into the relationship between educational theories, professional development and classroom practice. In particular, an exploration of the articulation and promulgation of distinctive types of educational and pedagogical theory through teacher training courses and its subsequent transmission to schools through teachers will be instructive. This rhetoric–reality dilemma, which turns on the 'notorious difference between what a teacher considers desirable in the seclusion of his study and what he considers possible in the hurly-burly of the classroom' (Selleck, 1968: 27), inevitably raises difficult methodological and source-based problems for historians. However, such difficulties can be surmounted with more creative, flexible and inter-disciplinary approaches to educational history.

Having explored the closely related themes of teacher training and pedagogy, it is fitting that the implications of recent policy on professional identity should be considered. Over the last 20 years serving teachers have been subjected to endless criticism and attacks on their professional integrity as they have been forced to adapt to the ever-shifting goalposts of the National Curriculum, local management of schools, testing and accountability, OFSTED inspections and league tables. Indeed, this tendency towards what is colloquially known as 'teacher bashing' has become ingrained into today's social and political culture. Naturally, constant attacks on teacher professionalism make teachers feel devalued. Research suggests that a coherent sense of professional identity remains an area of real difficulty for teachers, with many experiencing profound identity confusion (Nias, 1989; Hirsh, 1993; Maclure, 1993). This crisis of identity and career might be explained in terms of a persistent, ongoing struggle on the part of school teachers to gain proper recognition of their professional status alongside the more traditional professions of, for example, medicine and law. Long-held aspirations for self-regulation and professional independence have finally been realized with the setting up of the General Teaching Council in September 2000. This particular battle in itself has a long and complicated history (for example Baron, 1954; Ross, 1990; Willis, 1996). The Green Paper of 1998 on the modernization of the profession announced government plans to introduce performance-related pay (Department for Education and Employment, 1998a). This proposal, whose roots can be found in the much-hated 'payment by results' system of the nineteenth century, paid little attention to the hard-won lessons of history. Teacher morale is understandably very low, and recruitment to the profession has become increasingly problematic.

Now that teaching, learning and pedagogy have moved to centre stage in the political arena, contested notions of professional expertise, as well as the relationship between the State and teaching, have been left open to question. Clearly, policy-makers have little faith in the so-called professional 'experts' – those teachers who work daily at the chalkface and those teacher trainers and educational researchers who are supposed to have an intimate knowledge and understanding of pressing educational concerns. Arguably, the introduction of a narrow, competence-based approach to teaching attacks teacher independence and professional integrity. The imposition of a highly mechanistic and technicist pedagogical discourse not only erodes professional identity on an individual level, but also indicts the teaching profession as a whole for its long history of apparently failing schools and children. The case for systematic research and development programmes to uphold, substantiate and promote a truly pedagogical approach to school learning has been argued more fully elsewhere (for example Wilkin, 1996; Goodson, 1997). Yet, the current political climate pays little heed to the contribution of educational research. All of this makes for a decidedly gloomy short-term future for teachers, teacher educators and educational researchers alike.

Many teachers, resisting the current wave of change, oppose what they consider to be a dehumanized, remote and unrealistic approach to classroom strategies and instructional methodologies. Just as it was earlier suggested that it is the historical gaps between the rhetoric and reality of educational theory in relation to educational practice which need to be re-examined for a deeper understanding of the pedagogical process, it can also be said that there are, and indeed will be, inevitable gaps between the imposition and implementation of educational policy-making (Alexander, Willcocks and Nelson, 1996: 117). It is in these gaps, however small, that teachers might still be able to exercise their professional judgment and find their professional voice. Historical research on the development of the teaching profession has suggested a hidden pattern of sustained teacher resistance towards certain prescribed policies and practices (for example Ozga and Lawn, 1982; Lawn, 1987; Oram, 1996). More research and a continued historical evaluation of the way in which teachers have interpreted the gulfs between policy and practice will undoubtedly enrich our present understanding of the perceived crisis in teachers' professional identity.

An integral part of this long historical continuum of teacher professionalism centres on the inescapably gendered nature of the world of schools and school teaching. Women have long dominated school teaching, particularly at primary level, and this has had a profoundly negative influence on attitudes and expectations towards the schooling of young children and the status of the teaching profession in general. In schools professional roles continue to be unevenly distributed among men and women, with men dominating in responsibility posts. This phenomenon sits uneasily alongside a shifting gender balance within society and, in more recent years, within higher education. Whilst there is growing literature on the implications of a feminized teaching profession to be found amongst broader feminist scholarship (for example Partington, 1976; Widdowson, 1980; Acker, 1989; Biklen, 1996; Copelman, 1996; Miller, 1996), there is scope for further, more integrated detailed historical study in this field. In particular, as we seek to understand and explain notions of contested professionalism, professionalization and identity, a much closer, contextualized examination of stereotypes, representations and assumptions about the position, quality and status of women teachers is required.

Throughout this chapter it has been argued that recent and current policy-making affecting teachers and teacher training has been born out of a very immediate and short-term view of education. The historical perspective, which locates present concerns within a much longer pattern of change and continuity, can temper and inform the current trend for seeking reactionary and novel solutions to age-old educational problems. Instead of automatically disregarding our professional heritage as at best irrelevant and at worst totally misguided, it is incumbent upon the State and its agencies to break this cycle of ignorance and neglect and to take a longer historical view.

At the same time, historians of education must work hard to counter the ill effects of over-simplified and sensationalist interpretations of past educational practices, which so often permeate current educational commentaries. Stereotyped caricatures of the 'bad old days' of Victorian schooling, when the cane reigned supreme, teachers were poorly educated and children were fed a meagre diet of basic reading, writing and arithmetic or, indeed, the 'good old days' when standards were supposedly high, order and discipline well maintained and teachers knew their place are all too familiar in both the popular and the educational press. These versions of history are not only misinformed, but they also perpetuate a damaging tradition of hostility towards the teaching profession and the culture of schooling. As has been suggested elsewhere (for example Cunningham and Gardner, 1997; Gardner, 1998) historians of education have an important role to play in redressing this balance.

Recent educational policy-making directed towards teaching and teacher training may be characterized in three ways. First, the increasingly centralized control of teaching and teacher training has placed the State in a much more dominant relation to the profession than it might previously have enjoyed. Secondly, there has been a definite move towards a much more mechanical, technicist discourse of teacher training and pedagogical practice. Finally, a steady devaluing of teachers' capabilities, autonomy and independence has left a legacy of professional discontent. Looking back to the history of ideas, methods and practices concerning teaching and learning in schools as well as the critical relationship between educational theory and practice begs a fundamental question. Is it possible for policy-makers to take something from our historical past as they seek to answer today's and tomorrow's educational problems? It is hoped that this chapter has demonstrated the potential for a revisited history of teacher training, pedagogy and professional identity to make a valuable contribution to future educational policy. The long-term consequences of such policy for teachers, schools and the nation's children are as yet unknown but, if historical enquiry continues to flourish in the new millennium, these will undoubtedly feature in any future historical research.

5 A contested and changing terrain: history of education in the twenty-first century

Richard Aldrich

Introduction

This chapter starts from the premise that history of education is, always has been, and always will be, a contested and changing terrain. My purpose, therefore, is to identify the terrain and to explain and analyse such contest and change. There is no intention to prescribe this or that solution for historians of education in the twenty-first century. Historians cannot predict the future with certainty. However, explanation and analysis of the contested and changing terrain that has been history of education until now may help us to understand both the present situation and future possibilities. Three preliminary points are made here by way of introduction. The first concerns the origins of the title of the chapter. The second raises some issues about the nature of history. The third introduces the concept of terrain.

The title is drawn from two substantial articles of a historical nature included in the December 1997 edition of *Educational Researcher*. The first, by Ellen Condliffe Lagemann, was entitled 'Contested terrain: a history of education research in the United States, 1890–1990'; the second, by Thomas K. Popkewitz, 'A changing terrain of knowledge and power: a social epistemology of educational research' (Lagemann, 1997; Popkewitz, 1997). Neither of these pieces, however, was specifically concerned with history of education in a narrow sense. Lagemann provided an historical overview of educational research in America over the past 100 years. Popkewitz went back to the beginning of the twentieth century to explore 'controversies about the knowledge of the social and educational sciences' (Popkewitz, 1997: 18).

The similarity of timeframe of the two studies may be explained by the general perception that modern social sciences, including the formal study of educational science in America (and in the United Kingdom), are a product of the late nineteenth century. Yet if there are similarities, there are also differences.

Lagemann's article is recognizably 'historical' in nature. Its basic organization is chronological, while tables provide statistical information on numbers of school pupils, teachers and principals, and of institutions and degrees in education across the period 1890–1990. Lagemann uses the theme of contest to organize her material, with a particular emphasis upon professionalization, which 'is seen as an ongoing competition to secure jurisdiction in particular domains of human service' (Lagemann, 1997: 5). Educational research is explained in terms of a series of contests between groups which include 'scholars of education, scholars in other fields and disciplines, school administrators, and teachers' (Lagemann, 1997: 5). Lagemann concludes that 'professionalization has been a barrier to the effective linking of knowledge and action in education' and looks forward to the development of 'more truly equal, genuinely respectful, and effectively collaborative relationships among the groups most directly involved in the study and practice of education' (Lagemann, 1997: 15).

Popkewitz's approach includes both historical and analytical strategies. He explains that the 'analysis draws on a broad band of conversations that I collectively call postmodern social and political theory' (Popkewitz, 1997: 18). His concept of a changing terrain is principally expressed neither in institutional nor professional terms. His is a 'messy' text which combines social, political and epistemological dimensions and uses:

> ... the concept of *register* to recognize that the present is composed of multiple and overlapping records – ideas, events, and occurrences that historically come together as the reason and rules of science .... My travelling among different sets of ideas is to think of them as part of a *scaffolding* – that is, to think of a grid or overlay of historically formed ideas whose pattern gives intelligibility to today's debates.
>
> (Popkewitz, 1997: 18)

The second introductory point concerns the nature of historical research and writing. The issue of 'what is history?' has been fiercely debated and recent influential publications on this theme have included those by Appleby, Hunt and Jacob (1994), Jenkins (1995) and Roberts (1997). Traditional narrative history which concentrates upon human beings and their motivation, experiences, actions, triumphs and failures, remains strong in Britain, not least in a field such as education. Geoffrey Elton, who died in December 1994, was the most powerful exponent of this philosophy of history. As a recent assessment has concluded:

> The cumulative result of Elton's efforts was a sustained defence of what may be called a human action account of the past; the view that history was not the result of social structures, objective forces or (as some post-modernists argue) linguistic discourses, but of autonomous human agents. To explain and comprehend the past, historians must provide an account of those agents' actions in their own terms, as they were lived and played out at the time. (Roberts, 1998: 29)

The two articles which prompted this chapter were written by American scholars and published in an American journal. Neither author is dismissive of individual human actions, but Lagemann locates the individuals in her account within their respective professional groups. Popkewitz emphasizes the extent to which the human sciences of the nineteenth century transformed individuals and events into data, and that debates about knowledge depend not only upon the debaters themselves but also upon the rules and conditions under which the debates take place. Clearly, human beings may exist within very limited and restrictive contexts – both ideological and institutional. They may act in concert rather than as individuals. But some narrative historians would no doubt be critical of Lagemann's approach on account of her single theory-based theme, while probably denying that Popkewitz's work constitutes history at all. No such concerns, however, intrude on the editorial introduction to the *Educational Researcher* in which the two articles appear. This editorial is headed 'Paradigm Differences in Historical Research'. While considerable emphasis is placed upon the different approaches of the two authors, for example 'whether theory is foregrounded or whether it is placed in the background and assigned a supporting role relative to historical evidence', there is no doubt in the editor's mind that both authors are historians and are writing history. Robert Donmoyer concludes: 'In short, the Lagemann and Popkewitz articles demonstrate that historical research is not immune to the sorts of paradigm differences and disputes that are commonplace in other fields and areas of study' (Donmoyer, 1997: 4).

A final comment needs to be made about the word 'terrain', which is used here to mean a field of activity – in this case the history of education. The issue of whether that field of activity is more properly characterized as a discipline is discussed in a later section. The terrain has several dimensions. The broadest and deepest is that of the educational activity of the human race stretching back to the beginning of time, and the memory or recording of that activity. Given that education is something which everyone has experienced, it is inhabited by virtually every human being in a private capacity, and by occupational groups such as politicians and journalists who would be more wary of intruding in other areas of professional knowledge such as medicine or engineering. Kenneth Baker (Secretary of State for Education, 1986–1989) reported that it was very difficult to get educational matters through Cabinet, 'because the one subject on which Cabinet Ministers love to digress in a very ill-formed way is reminiscing about their own school days' (*Times Educational Supplement*, 31 May 1996). This is but one example of the way in which, as Gary McCulloch has recently argued, the educational past has been privatized, often to the detriment of public, and more accurate versions of events (McCulloch, 1997b). The potential for the creation of a more public and accurate terrain stemmed from the development of history and of education as subjects of academic and professionalized study in the later nineteenth century.

The remainder of this chapter explores the themes of contest and change under three broad chronological headings. The first is the past – that which has already happened. The second is the present – that which is now. The third is the future – that which is yet to come.

The past

The historical study of education developed within two contexts: those of the academic subjects of history and of education. In respect of history, however, it did not develop very quickly nor did it acquire any particular identity. Historical study in the universities of the later nineteenth and earlier twentieth centuries was largely concerned with broad sweeps of British political history, together with more specialized studies of constitutional history, foreign policy and political thought. Education found little place in such studies, although historians were interested in the history of their own and other institutions of higher education, an interest that has continued to the present day.

In sharp contrast, the historical study of education within an educational context – the day training colleges introduced in the 1890s – was prescribed by the government. Under the terms of Circular 287, issued in May 1890, the government's direction of the staffing and curriculum of the new colleges was quite explicit: 'a normal master or mistress must be appointed to lecture on theory and history of education, to supervise teaching and to give a course of model lessons and preside at criticism lessons'. The history of education taught in these university colleges or departments included the history of British educational institutions, the 'rise of the schooled society', and the work of educational thinkers and reformers, from Plato to Arnold. Given that the audience was composed almost entirely of prospective teachers who were undertaking crowded courses which included a strong practical element in teaching practice, there was an understandable tendency for educational acts and facts and educational theories to become detached from their historical contexts.

History of education thus acquired its initial prominence and identity as a result of a more academic approach to the preparation of teachers in the 1890s. The second major period of development occurred in the 1960s and 1970s as teacher training colleges were transmuted into colleges of education and 2- and 3-year certificate courses were replaced by 3- and 4-year BEd degrees. History of education was strengthened in courses of initial and in-service teacher education. Basic texts in the subject sold in their thousands and hundreds flocked to the conferences of the History of Education Society. The formation of the British History of Education Society in 1967 marked a turning point in the contested and changing terrain. From this date forward, historians of education had a professional organization which was to produce a bulletin and journal and to hold regular conferences. Although, as William Richardson demonstrates in Chapter Two, some rapprochement between historians and educationists working in the field of history of education occurred in the period 1967–1976, since that date divergence has been the order of the day. The British History of Education Society has been organized and led by those in the Education rather than the History departments of higher education.

Connections between the two worlds of academic history and education had existed from the 1890s, and the publications of some of the earlier professorial historians of education based in Education departments, men such as Foster Watson and W.H. Woodward, won general approval. Only one Education chair, however, that held at King's College, London, was specifically linked with history, its first incumbent, J.W. Adamson (1903–1924) producing his magisterial volume, *English Education, 1789–1902*, in retirement in 1930. Adamson's successor in 1924, John Dover Wilson, was a notable Shakespearean scholar recruited from a post as one of His Majesty's Inspectors of Schools, who departed in 1933 to become Professor of Rhetoric and English Literature at the University of Edinburgh. The clearest connection between the worlds of history and of education occurred in 1949 when A.V. Judges, then reader in economic history at the London School of Economics, was appointed to the King's chair. Judges personified the link between the academic worlds of history and education. His successor, A.C.F. Beales (1964–1972) had fewer credentials as an historian. As editor of the *British Journal of Educational Studies* from its foundation in 1952 until his death in 1974, however, Beales commissioned many substantial and high-quality articles on historical topics in what rapidly became the most prestigious educational journal of its day. Beales, whose teaching duties at King's prior to his appointment to the chair had included lecturing on the English educational system and the preparation of history teachers for secondary schools, was mindful not only of the need for historians of education to retain strong contacts with the general world of history, but also with the general world of education. He remained wary of the History of Education Society, fearful that its conferences and publications would create a separate and isolated culture for historians of education.

Beales' concerns about the fragility of the connection between historians of education in Education departments and the academic world of history were soon confirmed. Forthright criticism of the History of Education Society appeared as early as 1969, when Gillian Sutherland of Newnham College, Cambridge, found the early discussions of the Society about the nature and purpose of history of education in colleges and institutes of higher education to be 'depressing' and concluded that 'It sounds as though the Society has yet to establish for itself the independent status and nature of historical enquiry' (Sutherland, 1969: 76).

Throughout the twentieth century, criticisms of the history of education as practised in institutions primarily devoted to the training and education of teachers were many and varied. These ranged from the lack of historical qualifications of many of those entrusted with the teaching of the subject, through the limited content of the curriculum – often characterized as 'acts and facts' – and its highly celebratory tone, to the misuse of history for the purpose of sharpening particular contemporary axes. Such criticisms have largely proceeded from an historical perspective. History of education has been criticized for not being good history. However, the current demise of history of education in the initial and in-service education and training of teachers has not occurred because it has been, or has been seen to have been, poor history. Its exclusion has depended upon a more general critique of academic and theoretical education. By the end of the 1980s, that exclusion in terms of one-year postgraduate courses of education was virtually complete, in spite of assertions by the then Secretary of State, Kenneth Baker, that 'Too many students spent far too long working on the theory and history of education and not nearly enough time learning how to handle a class or how to teach a subject in the classroom' (Aldrich, 1990b: 47–48). Teachers, it was argued, needed to be trained, not educated, for their professional role and to spend as much time as possible in schools. In consequence, the number of historians of education who are currently teaching the subject in Education departments is very small indeed. Insofar as the History of Education Society has largely recruited from this constituency, it appears to be catering for an ever diminishing and ageing clientele.

The present

The first task for historians of education today is to re-visit the question: what is history of education? Has there been a mismatch between history of education as it has developed in Britain and as exemplified by the History of Education Society on the one hand, and a better history of education exemplified in the work of academic historians on the other? How should the contest and change that has occurred since the 1890s be interpreted?

What is history of education? At first sight the answer seems to be clear. History of education is the historical study of education. History is the discipline – the means, the tool of study – and education is the field or area of study. Similarly, for example, the history of Africa is the historical study of Africa, or the history of Parliament the historical study of Parliament. History and historical study are characterized by several features. Some of these relate to the centrality of the distinctive dimension of time, indeed history may be defined as the study of human events with particular reference to the dimension of time. Others concern the nature of truth and the use of historical evidence. These characteristics serve to distinguish history from such disciplines as philosophy or psychology. They also serve to distinguish the history of education from the philosophy of education or the psychology of education, although substantial connections between such activities may frequently be made. Indeed, in the last decade of the nineteenth century when the subject of education began to acquire some place in universities, it was based in a theoretical sense upon the three foundations of: 'educational philosophy and principles, educational psychology, and the history of education from Plato onwards' (Beales, 1971: 132).

Two main challenges may be presented to this type of explanation of history of education.

The first is to question the distinction between a 'discipline' and a 'field of study'. Can the two be so confidently separated? Indeed, the *Longman Dictionary of the English Language* equates the two, and provides the following definition of a discipline: 'a subject that is taught, a field of study'. William Richardson began his two recent articles on 'Historians and educationists' with the statement that the essays 'examine the development since 1945 of the history of education as a field of study in England' (Richardson, 1999a: 1, 1999b: 109). Can a discipline also be a field of study depending upon its position as object rather than subject? For example, would a history of psychology or of physics transform the disciplines of psychology and physics into fields of study? Would the same apply to a history of sociology? And what of a sociology of history? Would history then become a field of study? Is the history of sociology (or the sociology of history) to be counted as the application of a discipline to a field of study or the application of one discipline to another discipline? Can a subject such as history (or indeed education) be operating as a discipline in some contexts and as a field of study in others?

A second question concerns developments in the nature and extent of human knowledge over time and space. Is it possible for a field of study at one period of time, or in one society, to acquire the status of a discipline in another? In 1969 Richard Szreter provided an interesting analysis of history, sociology and education. History, he described as a discipline, on the grounds that it 'is a relatively self-contained branch of knowledge in that the bulk of its subject-matter is not claimed by any other branch of knowledge, and its method has been evolved by its own practitioners and is largely peculiar to it' (Szreter, 1969: 85). Szreter acknowledged that sociology had some of the characteristics of a discipline – university departments, specialist courses of study, significant body of findings and specialist literature. He concluded, however, that sociology was more of a perspective and 'less of a separate discipline in virtue of what sociologists investigate and how they go about it' (Szreter, 1969: 85–86). Although education might be characterized as enjoying at least three, and possibly all four of the characteristics attributed by Szreter to sociology, he concluded that it was 'neither a discipline nor a perspective, but a *field of studies*' (Szreter, 1969: 86). The use of the plural is interesting and important, and indeed the very breadth and pervasiveness of education means that it may be both dangerous and inaccurate to denote it as a single field of study, let alone a discipline.

In 1971 this point was developed in an article in *Daedalus* by J.E. Talbott who 'doubted whether education, a process so deeply entangled in the life of an entire society, deserves to be called an "area of study" at all' (Talbott, 1971: 156). Although Szreter cited the historian of education, Brian Simon, and the sociologist of education, Jean Floud, in support of the centrality of formal education in their respective studies (Szreter, 1969: 87), Talbott argued that:

> Surely there can be little justification for making education a particular genre of historical scholarship. The history of education touches upon all the varieties of history. It is a task for the generalist, who must bring to the study of education a thorough knowledge of the society of which it is a part. (Talbott, 1971: 156)

This assertion was strongly challenged by Kenneth Charlton, who argued that politics, economics and religion were examples of other processes which were deeply entangled within the life of an entire society, and therefore might equally be reserved to the generalist historian. Some division of labour and specialization in historical studies was necessary. There would always be a need both for lumpers and for splitters. He concluded that 'as historians we legitimately concentrate our historical skills on a part of human experience, whilst retaining an awareness of the other parts' (Charlton, 1983: 8). The further point is that if education is so essential to the functioning of society, as Bailyn, Cremin, Talbott and others have argued, it is both curious and hugely disappointing that it has been so systematically excluded from the concerns of generalist historians and the pages of general histories.

As the above discussion indicates, there is no absolute and unchanging entity called history of education. It is an area of contest and change.

Much of the contest has been couched in terms of historians operating from the security of an established discipline criticizing those whose historical work is considered to be of lower status, because it is in some way contaminated by the priorities and concerns of the broad field of study, or studies, which currently constitutes education. History itself is a site of contest and change, but not so much as education. Nor are its contests and changes so immediate in terms of the future of history of education. It may be that history of education will disappear from Education departments and find its main location in History departments. In that case, its future identity will be construed within the context of debates about the nature of history. However, at present the great debates in the United Kingdom are about education and now, and possibly for the first decade of the twenty-first century, the nature and purpose of history of education has to be considered within that context. Geoffrey Elton was wont to distinguish between on the one hand situational causes, the background or contexts, and on the other direct causes, the human actions which produce both contest and change. The situational causes in this instance are the educational reforms of the Conservative governments of 1979–1997, including the focus on school-based training for teachers, and the current Labour government's emphases on standards and on the centrality of teachers in the raising of such standards. The potential for direct action and the promotion of direct cause for historians of education lies in the contributions they can make to the development of the academic subject of education in general and to the solution of the current problems identified by government of raising of standards of attainment of school pupils and the recruitment and retention of good teachers. Of course, it is possible, even probable, as William Richardson points out, that if historians of education focus their attention on providing a 'usable past' to current practitioners and policy-makers, their work will continue to be dismissed by some academic historians. However, as I have argued elsewhere, the choice is not simply between using or not using the past in deciding upon current and future courses of action, but between drawing upon versions of the past which are of a manifestly unsatisfactory and inaccurate nature and those which demonstrate a greater correspondence with reality (Aldrich, 1997: 7–12).

Contest and change in respect of education, including its academic and professional elements, is a worldwide phenomenon, heightened perhaps by the diminution as a result of globalization in control which governments can now exercise over such areas as foreign and financial policies. The problem, however, does seem to be particularly acute within the UK, where the contraction of spheres of power and influence has been exacerbated by the end of empire and relative economic decline, and especially in England. As Marie-Madeleine Compère has argued, in England 'education in its proper sense, however, has never enjoyed any great intellectual prestige and thus has no inertia to set against historical innovation, as might be the case if it possessed a prestigious tradition' (Compère, 1993: 243). The causes of this low status are many and varied. For example, Jon Lauglo has drawn attention to the problems of rural primary school teachers in England in the second half of the nineteenth century, arguing that they lacked the status accorded to their contemporaries in many other European countries and were invariably subservient to the greater intellectual and social prestige of the Anglican clergy (Lauglo, 1982: 233–255). As for the status of the academic subject known as education, many commentators have remarked on its general 'immaturity'. Not only is it barely 100 years old as a subject of university study in modern Britain, but throughout that period it has been of low status – its staff and students generally holding lower academic qualifications and having higher percentages of females than those in other subjects, its courses subject to regulation and inspection by central government. As indicated above, it lacks standing as a discipline and one historian, Robert Skidelsky, has argued that 'education is also immature in the sense that what ought to be questions of fact are too often turned into questions of interpretation' (*Times Educational Supplement*, 4 February 1994). David Hargreaves has provided an explanation of this phenomenon in terms of the inadequate nature of much educational research, which he characterizes as 'non-cumulative, in part because few researchers seek to create a body of knowledge which is then tested, extended or replaced in some systematic way' (Hargreaves, 1996: 2).

Historians of education are well equipped to address such charges of immaturity and absence of a body of knowledge. The application of historical perspectives does enable some of the qualities and practices which have stood the test of time to be identified. Recognition of this possibility has meant that in the 1990s historians of education have been successful in securing grants for funded research in education. Recent examples at the Institute of Education, University of London, include a cultural and historical study of the Department for Education and Employment and an historical study of education welfare provision in London. Opportunities for this type of work appear to be on the increase, even in the pronouncements of those who are located at the opposite end of the educational spectrum. For example, Chris Woodhead, the current Chief HMI, is no particular friend of university departments of education nor of educational research. His recent statement, however, that in terms of educational research 'the future lies, if it lies anywhere, in rediscovering the importance of historical perspective' (*Independent*, 9 April 1998), provides one useful starting point for historians of education. Another is to be found in his OFSTED annual lecture, 'The Rise and Fall of the Reflective Practitioner', delivered on 23 February 1999. On that occasion, Woodhead argued against the concept of radical new roles for teachers and new pedagogies for the twenty-first century 'because nobody has yet been able to persuade me that (IT aside) the role will change' (Woodhead, 1999: 4). Historians of education are uniquely qualified to identify the continuities, contests and changes in the role of teachers and of teaching across the centuries.

The future

What of the future? Two points may be made. The first relates to the role of historians of education in respect of the education and training of members and prospective members of the teaching profession. The second is concerned with the production of knowledge, and in particular with the development of a discipline of education.

The first is to revisit Lagemann's conclusions about professionalization. Her call for a closer co-operation between the several professional groups engaged in education is a timely one, and can be justified by an extended analysis of professionalization. Rivalry between different professional groups in education in the United Kingdom, as in America, may well have been a major barrier to the effective linking of theory and practice and to the development of education as a discipline. Divisions in the United Kingdom have been only too marked – even within schools, which historically have been divided, along with their teachers, upon lines of social class and gender. This interpretation, however, must be combined both with a broader background and with a specific contemporary analysis. Professionals and professional groups cannot simply be seen as a problem. The professionalization of British society in the nineteenth and twentieth centuries – in central and local government as well as in the traditional and emerging professions – was essential to the creation of a more affluent, efficient and just society. However, as Harold Perkin, the major historian of this process, has argued, 'The triumph of the Thatcherites in Britain, like that of the Reaganites and Gingrich Republicans in the United States, was the victory of the private sector professionals over the rest of society' (Perkin, 1996: xiv). This triumph has been all too evident in the increasing gaps between rich and poor, the inflated, self-awarded salaries, bonuses and other perks paid to some in big business and commerce, the underfunding of public services, including the dismantling of the Welfare State. It is time for the public sector professionals in such areas as education and health to reassert the principles which have characterized, and should continue to characterize, the best elements in such services. In the year 2000 there are General Teaching Councils in England and Wales, to complement that which has long existed in Scotland. Historians of education can play an important role in this process of enhancing professional confidence and expertise by providing a nuanced and cumulative context for the distillation of the best of educational theory and practice at particular points in history, both past and present. In the 1890s history of education was introduced into the initial training of teachers by central government; by the 1990s the same agency had ensured its demise. The prospect of a profession in which teachers themselves have a greater control over their own initial and in-service education and training provides an opportunity for historians of education to state their claims to contribute to such education and training.

The second point is concerned with identity. In the terminology of Popkewitz, the history of the twenty-first century, in common with all history that has gone before, will indeed be a messy text, as information technology places increasing power at the finger tips of individuals whose identities are neither given nor constrained by their location or type of employment at any one time in their lives. Former identities and divisions will be contested and challenged. For example, Richardson recently concluded his articles on 'Historians and educationists' with the statement that there is a

> ... long-standing and defining difference between the practice in England (and overseas) of academic historians who reconstruct the past in ways influenced by present concerns and of educationists who invoke the past in order to apply its lessons to present concerns. In the study of the history of education this has, since the 1930s at least, entailed a broad division of labour between those in history departments interested in the influence of education on society and those in the education departments interested in the influence of society on education.
> (Richardson, 1999b: 138)

Such differences may, indeed, have existed to some degree, but it is also clear that most history of education written by historians located in the Education departments of universities has not been concerned with invoking the past in order to apply its lessons to present concerns. Richardson is also in error in respect of such basic matters of fact as the date of this author's professorial appointment and the numbers of the Institute of Education's MA students (Richardson, 1999b: 133). Richardson's very use of the terms 'educationists' and 'academic historians' (Richardson, 1999a: 3) in contradistinction to each other, must also be contested. For example, Gary McCulloch, contributor to this volume and the editor of the very journal in which Richardson's articles appeared, is an 'academic historian', although based in the Division of Education at the University of Sheffield. Charlton's explanation of the relationship between the two roles is illuminating:

> As professional historians involved in the teaching of history of education as part of the professional education of teachers, we ourselves *study* history of education in exactly the same way as any other professional historian, imposing upon our study and writing exactly the same self-denying ordinance. When we teach history of education as part of professional education we have a different (though not totally different) responsibility and aim from those of our colleagues who, for example, teach history (of whatever kind, including history of education) to undergraduate students who are not being prepared for entry to the teaching profession. (Charlton, 1983: 9–10)

The twenty-first century, with its changing terrain of knowledge and power, also provides the prospect of teaching education to undergraduate students who are not being prepared for entry to the teaching profession. Of course, we are all constrained by the various contexts within which we live, and historians in Education departments of universities have been more clearly constrained by government intervention than have those in History departments. Yet such constraints have related essentially to the role of education as a subject in the professional preparation of school teachers.

Changes in identity will continue to occur in higher education. As yet, the amount of research and writing undertaken by generalists and other historians in the History departments of institutions of higher education has been less than that produced by Education departments. The recent emphasis upon school-based initial teacher training and the decline of the 'disciplines' might seem to presage a change in this situation, but it is also possible that education as a subject of undergraduate and postgraduate study for those who do not intend to become teachers will become at least as important a subject of study as history. For if education is indeed as central a theme in human existence as Bailyn, Talbott and others have argued, then it is a proper study for subject in universities. As such, it may indeed move from its current status as a field or fields of study towards that of a recognized discipline.

Thus, historians of education may draw from Lagemann and Popkewitz the concept of a changing and contested terrain, both in respect of history and of education, and from Elton that 'direct causes in history are, fundamentally, human chains of action and reaction which can be reconstructed from evidence' (Roberts, 1998: 30). The evidence suggests that in the twenty-first century the ideal and concept of lifelong learning will transform both the nature and practice of education and of its history.

References

Acker, S. (1989), *Gender and careers*. London: Falmer.
Aldrich, R. (1990a), 'The evolution of teacher education'. In N. Graves (ed.) *Initial Teacher Education: Policies and Progress*. London: Kogan Page, 12–24.
Aldrich, R. (1990b), 'History of education in initial teacher education in England and Wales'. *History of Education Society Bulletin*, 45, 47–53.
Aldrich, R. (1993), 'Discipline, policy and practice: a personal view of the history of education'. In K. Salimova and E. Johanningmeier (eds) *Why should we teach the history of education?* Moscow: Rusanov Publishing House, 141–154.
Aldrich, R. (1996), *Education for the nation*. London: Cassell.
Aldrich, R. (1997), *The end of history and the beginning of education*. London: Institute of Education, University of London.
Aldrich, R., Crook, D. and Watson, D. (2000), *Education and employment: the DfEE and its place in history*. London: Institute of Education, University of London.
Alexander, R., Willcocks, J. and Nelson, N. (1996), 'Discourse, pedagogy and the national curriculum: change and continuity in primary schools'. *Research Papers in Education Policy and Practice* 11, 1, 81–120.
Appleby, J., Hunt, L. and Jacob, M. (1994), *Telling the truth about history*. New York: Norton.
Armytage, W. (1953), 'The place of the history of education in training courses for teachers'. *British Journal of Educational Studies* 1. In P. Gordon and R. Szreter (eds) (1989), *History of education: the making of a discipline*. London: Woburn, 47–54.
Bailyn, B. (1960), *Education and the formation of American society*. Chapel Hill: North Carolina University Press.
Bailyn, B. (1963), 'Education as a discipline: some historical notes'. In J. Walton and J. Kuethe (eds), *The discipline of education*. Madison: University of Wisconsin Press, 125–139.

References

Baker, K. (1993), *The turbulent years: my life in politics*. London: Faber and Faber.
Barger, R. and Barger, C. (1998), 'Teaching and learning history of education through the World Wide Web'. ISCHE XX conference paper, published online at http://www.nd.edu/~rbarger/ische98.
Barnett, C. (1986), *The audit of war: the illusion and reality of Britain as a great nation*. London: Macmillan.
Baron, G. (1954), 'The teachers' registration movement'. *British Journal of Educational Studies*, 2, 2, 134–144.
Bassey, M. (1992), 'Creating education through research'. *British Education Research Journal*, 18, 1, 3–16.
Batho, G. (1983), 'The current situation in the teaching of the history of education in diplomas, masters taught courses and research degrees'. In R. Lowe (ed.), *Trends in the study and teaching of the history of education*. Leicester: History of Education Society, 48–60.
Beales, A. (1971), 'The place of the history of education in the training of teachers'. In J. Higginson (ed.) *Gleanings for tomorrow's teachers*. In P. Gordon and R. Szreter (eds) (1989), *History of education: the making of a discipline*. London: Woburn, 131–142.
Biklen, S. (1996), *School work: gender and the cultural construction of teaching*. New York: Teachers' College Press.
Blackman, J. and Neld, K. (1976), 'Editorial'. *Social History*, 1, 1–3.
Board of Education (1926), *The education of the adolescent (Hadow report)*. London: HMSO.
Briggs, A. (1972), 'The study of the history of education'. *History of Education*, 1, 1. In P. Gordon and R. Szreter (eds) (1989), *History of education: the making of a discipline*. London: Woburn, 160–175.
Callaghan, J. (1987), *Time and chance*. London: Collins.
Cannadine, D. (1987), 'British history: past, present – and future?'. *Past and Present*, 116, 169–191.
Carter, J. (1996), 'Writing university history for Aberdeen's quincentenary'. *History Today*, 45, 2, 7–9.
Charlton, K. (1983), '"The benefit of the rear-view mirror": history of education in the professional education of teachers'. In R. Lowe (ed.) *Trends in the study and teaching of the history of education*. Leicester: History of Education Society, 3–13.
Clark, J. (1988), 'What is social history?'. In J. Gardiner (ed.) *What is history today ... ?* London: Macmillan, 51–52.
Clarke, K. (1992), 'Education's insane bandwagon finally goes into the ditch'. *Sunday Times*, 26 January.

Cohen, S. (1976), 'The history of the history of education, 1900–1976: uses of the past'. *Harvard Educational Review*, 43, 6, 298–330.

Cohen, S. (1977), 'The history of education in the United States: historians of education and their discontents'. In D. Reeder (ed.) *Urban education in the nineteenth century*. London: Taylor and Francis, 115–132.

Compère, M.-M. (1993), 'Textbooks on the history of education currently in use in Europe'. In K. Salimova and E. Johanningmeier (eds) *Why should we teach history of education?* Moscow: Rusanov Publishing House, 236–244.

Copelman, D. (1996), *London's women teachers: gender, class and feminism 1870–1930*. London: Routledge.

Cremin, L. (1970), *American education: the colonial experience, 1607–1783*. New York: Harper and Row.

Crook, D. (1999), 'Viewing the past: the treatment of history of education on British television since 1985'. *History of Education*, 28, 3, 365–369.

Cunningham, P. (1989), 'Educational history and educational change: the past decade of English historiography'. *History of Education Quarterly*, 29, 1, 77–94.

Cunningham, P. and Gardner, P. (1997), 'Editorial'. *Cambridge Journal of Education*, 27, 3, 309–311.

Davies, B. (1994), 'On the neglect of pedagogy in educational studies and its consequences'. *British Journal of In-Service Education*, 20, 1, 17–34.

Dent, K. (1983), 'The relevance of the rear-view mirror in initial training'. In R. Lowe (ed.) *Trends in the study and teaching of the history of education*. Leicester: History of Education Society, 29–47.

Department for Education and Employment (1997), *Excellence in schools*. London: Stationery Office.

Department for Education and Employment (1998a), *Teachers: meeting the challenge of change*. London: Stationery Office.

Department for Education and Employment (1998b), *The learning age: a renaissance for a new Britain*. London: Stationery Office.

Department of Education and Science (1979), *Developments in the BEd course*. London: DES.

Department of Education and Science (1991), *Education and training for the 21st century*. Volume one. London: HMSO.

Donmoyer, R. (1997), 'Paradigm differences in historical research'. *Educational Researcher*, 26, 9, 4.

'Editorial Collective' (1976), 'Editorial'. *History Workshop Journal*, 1, 1–3.

Elliott, J. (1997), 'Quality assurance, the educational standards debate and the commodification of educational research'. *The Curriculum Journal*, 8, 1, 63–83.

Elton, G. (1969), 'Second thoughts on history at the university'. *History*, 54, 60–67.

References

Evans, R. (1997), *In defence of history*. London: Granta.

Finkelstein, B. (1992), 'Educational historians as mythmakers'. In G. Grant (ed.) *Review of research in education*. Washington DC: American Educational Research Association, 255–297.

Fullan, M. (1993), *Change forces: probing the depths of educational reform*. London: Falmer.

Galton, M. and Simon, B. (eds) (1980), *Progress and performance in the primary classroom*. London: Routledge and Kegan Paul.

Galton, M., Simon, B. and Croll, P. (1980), *Inside the primary classroom*. London: Routledge and Kegan Paul.

Gardner, P. (1993), 'The early history of school-based teacher training'. In D. Macintyre, H. Hagger and M. Wilkin (eds) *Mentoring: perspectives on school-based teacher education*. London: Kogan Page, 21–36.

Gardner, P. (1996), 'Higher education and teacher training: a century of progress and promise'. In J. Furlong and R. Smith (eds) *The role of higher education in initial teacher training*. London: Kogan Page, 35–49.

Gardner, P. (1998), 'Classroom teachers and educational change 1876–1996'. *Journal of Education for Teaching*, 24, 1, 33–49.

Gay, P. (1975), *Style in history*. London: Cape.

Goodman, J., Martin, J. and Robinson, W. (1998), 'Editorial: retrospect and prospect'. *History of Education Society Bulletin*, 61, 1–7.

Goodson, I. (1997), '"Trendy theory" and teacher professionalism'. *Cambridge Journal of Education*, 27, 1, 7–23.

Gosden, P. (1981), 'Twentieth century archives of education as sources for the study of education policy and administration'. *Archives*, 15, 66, 86–95.

Gosden, P. (1983), 'Recent developments in the study of the history of education in teacher-education courses'. In R. Lowe (ed.) *Trends in the study and teaching of the history of education*. Leicester: History of Education Society, 14–19.

Graham, J. (1996), 'Closing the circle: research, critical reflection and the national curriculum for teacher training'. *Higher Education Review*, 29, 1, 33–56.

Graham, J. (1997), 'The national curriculum for teacher training: playing politics or promoting professionalism?' *British Journal of In-Service Education*, 23, 2, 163–177.

Hargreaves, D. (1996), *Teaching as a research-based profession: possibilities and prospects*. TTA annual lecture. London: TTA.

Harrison, B. (1968), 'History at the universities'. *History*, 53, 357–380.

Hillage, J. (1998), *Excellence in research on schools*. London: Institute of Employment Studies.

Hirsh, G. (1993), 'Biography and teacher identity: a typological analysis of life-history data'. *Qualitative Studies in Education*, 6, 1, 67–83.

Howard, M. (1981), *The lessons of history*. Oxford: Oxford University Press.
Hurt, J. (1975), 'Bibliographical essay'. *Bulletin of the Society for the Study of Labour History*, 30, 42–54.
Jenkins, K. (1995), *On 'what is history?' from Carr and Elton to Rorty and White*. London: Routledge.
Katz, M. (1987), *Reconstructing American education*. London: Harvard University Press.
Lagemann, E. (1997), 'Contested terrain: a history of education research in the United States, 1890–1990'. *Educational Researcher*, 26, 9, 5–17.
Lauglo, J. (1982), 'Rural primary teachers as potential community leaders? Contrasting historical cases in western countries'. *Comparative Education*, 18, 3, 233–255.
Lawn, M. (1987), *Servants of the State: the contested control of teaching, 1900–1930*. London: Falmer.
Layton, D. (1973), *Science for the people: the origins of the school science curriculum in England*. London: George Allen and Unwin.
Lowe, R. (1983), 'History as propaganda: the strange uses of the history of education'. In R. Lowe (ed.) *Trends in the study and teaching of the history of education*. In P. Gordon and R. Szreter (eds) (1989), *History of education: the making of a discipline*. London: Woburn, 225–240.
McCulloch, G. (1994), *Educational reconstruction: the 1944 education act and the 21st century*. London: Woburn.
McCulloch, G. (1996), 'Educating the public: Tawney, the *Manchester Guardian* and educational reform'. In R. Aldrich (ed.) *In history and in education*. London: Woburn, 116–137.
McCulloch, G. (1997a), 'Marketing the millennium: education for the 21st century'. In A. Hargreaves and R. Evans (eds) *Beyond educational reform: bringing teachers back in*. Buckingham: Open University Press, 19–28.
McCulloch, G. (1997b), 'Privatising the past? History and education policy in the 1990s'. *British Journal of Educational Studies*, 45, 1, 69–82.
McCulloch, G. (1998a), 'Historical studies in science education'. *Studies in Science Education*, 31, 31–54.
McCulloch, G. (1998b), *Failing the ordinary child: the theory and practice of working-class secondary education*. Buckingham: Open University Press.
Maclure, M. (1993), 'Arguing for your self: identity as an organizing principle in teachers' jobs and lives'. *British Educational Research Journal*, 19, 4, 311–322.
Marshall, B. (1999), 'How to teach the teacher', *Independent*, 1 April.
Marwick, A. (1970), *The nature of history*. London: Macmillan.
Miller, J. (1996), *School for women*. London: Virago.

Millett, A. (1995), *Securing excellence in teaching*. TTA annual lecture. London: Teacher Training Agency.

Millett, A. (1996), *Pedagogy: the last corner of the secret garden*. TTA annual lecture. London: Teacher Training Agency.

Mortimore, P. (1998), 'Attack on educational research'. *Times Higher Educational Supplement*, 3 April.

Morton, A. (1997), *Education and the State from 1833* (Public Record Office Readers' Guide 18). Kew: PRO Publications.

National Commission on Education (1993), *Learning to succeed*. London: Heinemann.

Nias, J. (1989), *Primary teachers talking: a study of teaching as work*. London: Routledge.

Niblett, W.R., Humphreys, D.W. and Fairhurst, J.R. (1975), *The university connection*. Slough: NFER.

OFSTED (1993a), *The articled teacher scheme, September 1990–June 1992*. London: HMSO.

OFSTED (1993b), *The licensed teacher scheme, September 1990–July 1992*. London: HMSO.

OFSTED (1993c), *The new teacher in school: a survey by HMI in England and Wales*. London: HMSO.

Oram, A. (1996), *Women teachers and feminist politics*. Manchester: Manchester University Press.

Orme, N. (1973), *English schools in the middle ages*. London: Methuen.

Ozga, J. and Lawn, M. (1982), *Teachers, professionalism and class: a study of organized teachers*. Lewes: Falmer.

Partington, G. (1976), *Women teachers in the twentieth century*. Windsor: NFER.

Patrick, H., Bernbaum, G. and Reid, K. (1982), *The structure and process of initial teacher education within universities in England and Wales*. Leicester: University of Leicester School of Education.

Perkin, H. (1996), *The third revolution: professional elites in the modern world*. London: Routledge.

Perks, R. (1990), *Oral history: an annotated bibliography*. London: British Library.

Popkewitz, T. (1997), 'A changing terrain of knowledge and power: a social epistemology of educational research'. *Educational Researcher*, 26, 9, 18–30.

Pring, R. (1992), *Academic respectability and professional relevance*. Oxford: Clarendon.

Puttnam, Lord (1999), 'The uninformed society'. British Library Chadwyck-Healey Lecture, London, 23 June.

Reynolds, D. (1998a), 'Wanted: reliable self-starters'. *Times Educational Supplement*, 17 July.

Reynolds, D. (1998b), 'The need for a science of teaching'. *Times Higher Educational Supplement*, 31 July.

Richardson, W. (1999a), 'Historians and educationists: the history of education as a field of study in post-war England. Part 1: 1945–72'. *History of Education*, 28, 1, 1–30.

Richardson, W. (1999b), 'Historians and educationists: the history of education as a field of study in post-war England. Part 2: 1972–96'. *History of Education*, 28, 2, 109–141.

Roberts, G. (1997), 'Postmodernism versus the standpoint of action'. *History and Theory*, 36, 2, 249–260.

Roberts, G. (1998), 'Geoffrey Elton and the philosophy of history'. *The Historian*, 57, 29–31.

Robinson, W. (1997), 'The pupil–teacher centre in England and Wales in the late nineteenth and early twentieth centuries: policy, practice and promise'. Unpublished PhD thesis, University of Cambridge.

Ross, A. (1990), 'The control of teachers' education: a General Teaching Council for England and Wales'. In N. Graves (ed.) *Initial teacher education: policies and progress*. London: Kogan Page, 124–143.

Saslaw, R. and Hiner, N. (1993), 'What are we teaching in the history of education?' In K. Salimova and E. Johanningmeier (eds) *Why should we teach the history of education?* Moscow: Rusanov Publishing House, 245–263.

Seaborne, M. (1971), 'The history of education'. In J.W. Tibble (ed.) *An introduction to the study of education*. London: Routledge and Kegan Paul, 65–79.

Selleck, R. (1968), *The new education, 1870–1914*. London: Pitman.

Selleck, R. (1972), *English primary education and the progressives*. London: Routledge.

Silver, H. (1985), 'History in a policy field: a British chef in Paris?' *History of Education Review*, 14, 1, 1–11.

Silver, H. (1990), 'Is there a future in the past?' In H. Silver (ed.) *Education, change and the policy process*. London: Falmer, 5–18.

Simon, B. (1966), 'The history of education'. In J.W. Tibble (ed.) *The study of education*. In P. Gordon and R. Szreter (eds) (1989) *History of education: the making of a discipline*. London: Woburn, 55–72

Simon, B. (1981), 'Why no pedagogy in England?' In B. Simon (ed.) *Does education matter?* London: Lawrence and Wishart, 77–105.

Simon, B. (1990), 'The study of education as a university subject'. In J. Thomas (ed.) *British universities and teacher education*. London: Falmer.

Simon, B. and Willcocks, J. (eds) (1981), *Research and practice in the primary classroom*. London: Routledge and Kegan Paul.

Smithers, A. (1995), 'Let usefulness be our yardstick for research'. *Times Educational Supplement*, 8 September.

Smithers, A. (1997), 'View from here'. *Independent*, 18 September.
Stevenson, D. (1993), 'The end of history? The British university experience, 1981–92'. *Contemporary Record*, 7, 1, 66–85.
Stone, L. (1969), 'Literacy and education in England, 1640–1900'. *Past and Present*, 42, 69–139.
Sutherland, G. (1969), 'The study of the history of education'. *History*, 54. In P. Gordon and R. Szreter (eds) (1989), *History of education: the making of a discipline.* London: Woburn, 73–84.
Sutherland, G. (1973), *Policy-making in elementary education, 1870–1895.* Oxford: Oxford University Press.
Szreter, R. (1969), 'History and the sociological perspective in educational studies'. *University of Birmingham Historical Journal*, 12. In P. Gordon and R. Szreter (eds) (1989), *History of education: the making of a discipline.* London: Woburn, 85–104.
Talbott, J. (1971), 'The history of education'. *Daedalus*, 100. In P. Gordon and R. Szreter (eds) (1989), *History of education: the making of a discipline.* London: Woburn, 143–159.
Teacher Training Agency (1996), *Promoting excellence in teaching.* London: HMSO.
Thatcher, M. (1995), *The path to power.* London: Harper-Collins.
Thomas, K. (1976), *Rule and misrule in the schools of early modern England.* Reading: University of Reading.
Thompson, P. (2nd edition, 1988), *The voice of the past: oral history.* Oxford: Oxford University Press.
Tooley, J. with Darby, D. (1998), *Educational research: a critique.* London: OFSTED.
Tosh, J. (1984), *The pursuit of history: aims, methods and new directions in the study of modern history.* London: Longman.
van Setten, H. (1998), 'Sand dunes around the ivory tower: the image of education history through the Web' (ISCHE XX conference paper, published online at http://www.socsci.kun.nl/ped/whp/histeduc/edhistweb.html.
Webster, C. (1976), 'Changing perspectives in the history of education'. *Oxford Review of Education*, 2, 1. In P. Gordon and R. Szreter (eds) (1989), *History of education: the making of a discipline.* London: Woburn, 176–193.
Whitbread, N. (1968), 'History of education in the three year certificate course'. *History of Education Society Bulletin*, 1, 4–13.
Widdowson, F. (1980), *Going up into the next class: women and elementary school teaching, 1840–1914.* London: WRRC.
Wiener, M. (1981), *English culture and the decline of the industrial spirit, 1850–1980.* Cambridge: CUP.

Wilkin, M. (1996), *Initial teacher training: the dialogue of ideology and culture.* London: Falmer.

Willis, R. (1996), 'Professional autonomy or state sponsorship: the dilemmas for private teachers in their campaign for registration in Victorian England'. *History of Education*, 25, 4, 323–334.

Woodhead, C. (1997), 'Inspecting schools: the key to raising educational standards'. Lecture to Royal Geographical Society, London, 21 January.

Woodhead, C. (1998), 'Academia gone to seed'. *New Statesman and Society*, 20 March, 51–52.

Woodhead, C. (1999), 'The rise and fall of the reflective practitioner'. Unpublished OFSTED annual lecture.

Woods, P and Wenham, P. (1995), 'Politics and pedagogy: a case study in appropriation'. *Journal of Education Policy*, 10, 2, 119–141.

Young, M. (1998), 'Rethinking teacher education for a global future'. *Journal of Education for Teaching*, 24, 1, 51–62.